Health, well-being and social inclusion

Therapeutic horticulture in the UK

Joe Sempik, Jo Aldridge and Saul Becker

Supported by

First published in Great Britain in May 2005 by

The Policy Press
University of Bristol
Fourth Floor, Beacon House
Queen's Road
Bristol BS8 1QU
UK

Tel no +44 (0)117 331 4054
Fax no +44 (0)117 331 4093
E-mail tpp-info@bristol.ac.uk
www.policypress.co.uk

Reprinted 2005, 2008

Transferred to Digital Print 2010

ISBN 978 1 86134 725 1

A study of the use of social and therapeutic horticulture for promoting health, well-being and social inclusion for vulnerable adults carried out by Loughborough University, in association with Thrive.

Joe Sempik (BSc, MSc, PhD) is a Research Fellow in the Centre for Child and Family Research, Loughborough University. **Jo Aldridge** (BA, PhD) is a Research Fellow in the Department of Social Sciences, Loughborough University. **Saul Becker** (BA, MA, CQSW, PhD) is Professor of Social Care and Health at University of Birmingham.

Cover design by Qube Design Associates, Bristol
Cover photograph: kindly supplied by Jo Aldridge
Printed in Great Britain by Marston Book Services, Oxford

Contents

List of tables and figures

Tables

Figures

Foreword

Growing Together is the largest piece of research in social and therapeutic horticulture, and hence a landmark in the field. The research team from Loughborough University have worked with the charity Thrive to survey the numerous small and large projects in therapeutic horticulture in progress around the country, and then studied a number of these projects in depth. They have shown the value of photographic evidence in carrying out such studies, and convinced me, a lifelong sceptic, that gardening is indeed a worthwhile therapy, improving the physical and mental health and social skills of its users. Like all good research studies, this work leaves a number of questions unanswered, but it does point the way to further work that will include, I hope, direct randomised comparison of such therapy with control groups. The practical and ethical difficulties of such an approach are great, but not insurmountable.

All the information from studies to date makes it clear that gardening is good for you. The Growing Together research shows how it goes much further than that. It is not a trivial activity, but is the setting for a wide range of activities enabling social contact, exercise and group interaction, as well as providing the opportunities for addressing cognitive and physical impairments and for developing vocational skills – all the elements that lead to social inclusion.

The long association that people have had with plants and the environment, such as the national allotment movement, leaves no doubt that such interactions are beneficial socially, physically and mentally to all groups of vulnerable people.

Social and therapeutic horticulture should now be considered an important part of health and social care, comparable to any other care application. I hope that this excellent report will help to make this country known for its positive use of therapeutic gardening.

Sir Richard Thompson
February 2005

Acknowledgements

This report was prepared by the Research Team at Loughborough University, UK, as part of the 'Growing Together' project funded by the National Lottery Community Fund. 'Growing Together – Promoting Social Inclusion, Health and Well-being for Vulnerable Adults through the use of Horticulture and Gardening' is a collaboration between Loughborough University and the charity Thrive.

The authors would like to acknowledge the Big Lottery Fund for the financial support of this project under grant number RG 10024093.

The authors acknowledge the cooperation and collaboration of their colleagues at Thrive, especially Tim Spurgeon and Louise Finnis and the consultants on the project: John Ferris, Carol Norman, Bill Silburn and Linda Eggins.

The authors would also like to thank the members of the Project Advisory Group for their help and advice:

Jon Fieldhouse, Senior Occupational Therapist, South Bristol Assertive Outreach Team, Avon and Wiltshire Mental Health Partnership

Professor Tony Gatrell, Dean, Faculty of Arts and Social Sciences, Lancaster University

Ed Macalister-Smith, Chief Executive, Nuffield Orthopaedic Centre NHS Trust, Oxford

Elisabeth Standen, Disability Consultant

Judy Ling Wong, Director, Black Environment Network

Sir Richard Thompson, Trustee, Thrive; Consultant Physician, St Thomas' Hospital

Finally, the research team would like to thank all of the projects and individuals who took part in this research. Without their cooperation this study would not have been possible. Because of the need for confidentiality, however, their identities cannot be disclosed and any names used in quotes or case studies have been changed. All photographs published in this report are reproduced with the subjects' permission.

1 Introduction

Background to the research

The value of open space and gardens within the urban environment has been recognised for centuries, but recognition of the benefits of the *process* of gardening is more recent. Gardening and horticulture are now used around the world as a means of promoting health and well-being for a wide range of disadvantaged and vulnerable adults and young people and in a variety of different contexts, for example, occupational therapy. The UK charity Thrive (formerly known as the Society for Horticultural Therapy) has been active for over 25 years in promoting and supporting the use of horticulture for vulnerable people, and has developed and maintained a network and database of such gardening and horticultural projects in the UK. It has also highlighted the need for research-based evidence to provide guidance for the projects and to inform policy makers. Thus it enabled this, the first major study of social and therapeutic horticulture in the UK. Known as 'Growing Together – Promoting Social Inclusion, Health and Well-being for Vulnerable Adults through the use of Horticulture and Gardening' the research programme has examined the level of activity of gardening projects in the UK and their associated benefits to vulnerable adults.

The first part of the study reviewed the available literature on social and therapeutic horticulture (Sempik et al, 2003). It is envisaged that this review will be updated periodically as more research is carried out in the field and more evidence becomes available.

The second phase of the research focused on the gardening project network established by Thrive. Although more than 1,500 gardening and horticulture projects for vulnerable people had been identified by Thrive since 1997, it became clear that because of changes within projects, for example, fluctuations in staffing and funding, there had been a constant turnover of projects. Some had closed and others had been created. It also became clear that some of the entries on the original database of projects were not active ones but individuals interested in starting projects, lone gardeners and others. Thus, it was necessary to reassess the network of projects to establish the number of active projects in the UK, the client groups and so on. This survey also provided valuable information about the structure, management and activities of projects and these data are presented in Chapter 3 of this report.

The third part of the research was to evaluate the benefits and limitations of social and therapeutic horticulture by studying a selected sample of projects, and this work forms the main body of the study.

During the course of the research, and visits to a variety of different projects and interviews with many practitioners, the authors have observed and analysed many of the issues involved in the *practice* of social and therapeutic horticulture. These have been collated and published as *Growing together: A practice guide to promoting social inclusion through gardening and horticulture* (Sempik et al, 2005), a partner publication to this volume. This work would not have been possible without the cooperation and help of the practitioners and project organisers involved.

The literature

The review of the literature (Sempik et al, 2003) concluded:

> **The data presented in this literature review provide evidence for the effectiveness of horticulture and gardening in a number of different therapeutic settings. Experimental evidence from environmental psychology also supports a theoretical framework for therapeutic horticulture. Even though this evidence does exist there is a need for more research and the authors of this review acknowledge the observations of previous writers who have highlighted the scant amount of 'hard evidence' that exists in support of therapeutic horticulture. (Sempik et al, 2003, p 47)**

Many of the articles examined in the course of preparation of the review were descriptive accounts of gardening projects or anecdotal accounts of the benefits of participating in them. 'Hard evidence' was hard to come by and the only truly experimental work came from the field of environmental psychology. Garden projects, themselves, are not easy to study as many different individual activities take place at a project, and these also vary from project to project; the client groups are often made up of people with a mix of vulnerabilities or disabilities and the outcomes or benefits vary according to the individual and may also vary according to the aims of the project. Even when a single client group is present, difficulties can be encountered in carrying out a study protocol. For example, Milligan et al (2003) set out to compare the effects on the health of older people of allotment gardening with those attending a social club (or attending neither). Their intention was to recruit around 300 older people to the two activities (and to a control group) using a random sampling method from the lists of general practitioners. Unfortunately, they were unable to recruit sufficient participants to enable them to carry out a comparison of the interventions using a quantitative measure of quality of life (SF-36). However, using qualitative methods, including in-depth interviews and diary records, they were able to conclude that:

> **Participants noted that although, on occasion, they found that gardening helped their fitness and stamina, its key benefit was in improving their sense of mental well-being. These positive aspects to gardening activity occurred despite, in some cases considerable, age-related health problems and disabilities.... (Milligan et al, 2003, p 47)**

They also found that social contact, whether on the allotment or in the social club setting, was a "vital factor in enhancing the health and well-being of older people, whatever activity they are involved in" (Milligan et al, 2003, p 7). The practical experiences of Milligan and her co-workers contrast sharply with the theoretical 'blueprint' put forward by Frumkin (2004) for the study of nature and horticulture:

> **It would study well-defined populations with specific, well-defined health conditions, recruited in large numbers to achieve a high level of statistical power. It would use randomised controlled trials whenever possible, to study well-defined clinical interventions. Importantly, these would not be limited to horticultural therapy. Horticulture more broadly – access to, and contact with plants, in a variety of settings, formal and informal, intentional and casual – deserves careful study. In fact, nature contact more generally, including direct contact with plants, contact with animals, views of gardens and landscapes, and wilderness activities, deserves intensive health outcomes research. This research would assess health outcomes using accurate, reproducible, validated measures. It would control the bias and confounding that would otherwise prevent clear conclusions. (Frumkin, 2004, p 23)**

Although such a study design would provide 'clear conclusions' it is unlikely that it could be carried out in the context of an established gardening project. Rather, laboratory conditions would be necessary to enable and control specifically defined, reproducible interventions using plants, nature or horticulture. Indeed, Yamane and his co-workers (Yamane et al, 2004) used such an environment in their study of the physiological and emotional effects of horticultural activities:

> **The subjects were seated on a chair in a windowless room (3.2 x 2m) controlled at 22 ± 1°C, RH 60%, and 800 lx of continuous white fluorescent light. Horticultural activities were performed on a desk. (Yamane et al, 2004, p 38)**

The authors used electro-encephalogram (EEG) and electromyogram (EMG) recordings to show that activities with plants 'promoted relaxation' and that using flowering plants was more effective in reducing negative emotional feelings than non-flowering plants (measured using the 'Profile of Moods States', a Likert scale to rate how appropriately particular adjectives describe a subject's emotional state). Closely controlled experimental conditions were also used by Son and his associates (Son et al, 2004) to study the effects of viewing a plant on EEG activity and blood pressure of schizophrenic patients. They observed a reduction in systolic blood pressure and heart rate and a reduction in delta waves as measured by the EEG. This, they suggest, could be beneficial to the patients. The work cited above (Frumkin, 2004; Yamane et al, 2004; and Son et al, 2004) was presented at an international conference with the theme 'Expanding Roles for Horticulture in Improving Human Well-Being and Life Quality' (Toronto, Canada, 2002; see Relf, 2004). While these and some other authors used physiological measurements under laboratory conditions to investigate the effects of working with plants, others used results from interviews and questionnaires to examine the benefits of participation in gardening or gardening projects. For example, Unruh (2004) used in-depth interviews to examine the meaning of gardens and gardening to participants with cancer and to compare it with that of healthy participants. She concluded:

> **As a possible coping strategy for stressful life experiences, gardening has several important dimensions. The garden and the activities associated with gardening parallel the life process. The gardener has opportunities for control in the life process of the garden that in personal life may seem elusive. The seasonal nature of gardening recreates a cycle of growth, maturation and death. For these reasons, gardening, as contrasted with other leisure occupations such as music or art, may have particularly poignant meaning for people who are faced with serious health crises such as cancer. Nevertheless, the experience of gardening may also change if stress exceeds the capacity of the individual to find enjoyment in leisure activities, or if the person's interest or life circumstances change. (Unruh, 2004, p 71)**

Stigsdotter and Grahn (2004) used a questionnaire to investigate the role that private gardens may play in reducing stress. They found that people with access to a garden had statistically significant lower 'sensitivity to stress' (a measure of stress, irritation and fatigue) than those without access to a garden and that visiting the garden often had a positive impact on stress.

These studies all illustrate the ongoing nature of research in the area of plants, horticulture, health and well-being. At least two major approaches are present – an examination of the effects of discrete components of gardening projects in laboratory conditions and the evaluation of the effects of participation in such activities using qualitative methods and questionnaires. The first approach has similarities to the experimental work of environmental psychology and while it provides definitive answers to specific questions, there is a need to extrapolate the information gained in this way into the context of 'real' gardening or horticulture experiences and the promotion of health and well-being. This approach, therefore, investigates the 'efficacy' of being involved in horticulture or experiencing nature. Efficacy refers to the empirical validation of an intervention under controlled conditions. However, "there is more to determining whether an intervention is useful or valuable than demonstrating that it can produce a change under controlled conditions. Hence, the empirical validation of therapeutic interventions needs to extend to a demonstration of effectiveness in real world clinical settings" (Becker, 2004, p 52; see also Jadad, 1998, pp 13-14).

The second approach takes place in the true setting of horticulture and therefore explores effectiveness. It examines the perceptions and feelings of those involved in it. While these are subjective they provide a measure of the emotional effects of participation. Other, objective measures have also been used in this setting, for example, numbers of hospital admissions, academic achievement or employment rates.

These two approaches are complementary and highlight the need to use a variety of methods to study the health and well-being effects of participation in gardening and horticulture. They also highlight the need for the development of new methodologies that will be appropriate to the different client groups. For example, while there are many different questionnaires of health and well-being, few if any are useful in the case of clients who have poor communication abilities. Many of those who participate in specific horticulture programmes have such difficulties. Clients with mental health problems or learning difficulties make up the greatest proportion of participants at gardening projects. A flexible and adaptive approach is necessary particularly when clients with different abilities and vulnerabilities are present in the same project or group. These issues of methodology are discussed in the next chapter as the research presented in this report has looked at a wide range of organised horticulture projects for vulnerable adults and encountered participants with many different difficulties and challenges.

2 Methodology

In this chapter we focus on the methods used in our in-depth survey of social and therapeutic horticulture (STH) projects, data from which provide insight into the benefits of STH projects for a range of vulnerable groups and allow us to discuss in detail later in the report the implications for health and social care policy and practice in respect of the use and benefits of STH. We also present findings from the survey of projects in Thrive's network (Chapter 3, pp 22-36).

Sample selection

A purposive sampling method was used drawing on Thrive's database of known operational horticultural projects across the UK, and using Thrive's criteria for selection, that is, we included: 'successful projects that reflect the make-up of the network'. Five projects were identified for inclusion in the initial pilot study where research methods were tried and tested. A further 22 projects were selected and approached at a later date with a view to inclusion in the full investigation and these included projects with a diverse client base, wide geographical distribution and varying numbers of clients. A letter of introduction, which included information about the research team, the study and its aims, was distributed among the projects. Requests for participation in the study were also made in this introductory correspondence. Once participants had agreed to take part in the study, the research team made follow-up telephone calls to arrange access to projects and interviews with participants, and to discuss any further issues in respect of the interview process and methodology. Access was obtained to 19 of the 22 projects and a brief description of all 24 projects in the study is shown in Table 2.1.

Making contact

Initial telephone calls are often a crucial stage in the research process as they enable researchers to 'establish rapport' or build relationships of trust with participants (see Arksey, 1996). Even at such a preliminary stage, the extent to which 'rapport' can be established (in this case with project staff) can have considerable influence on whether full access to respondents is granted. Initial telephone contact, particularly in this case with project staff, meant any queries or problems relating to the study and access to project sites and participants could be identified and discussed early on.

Although access to most of the 24 projects in our study was unproblematic, gaining access to clients at some projects could not be arranged without an initial personal introductory 'visit' by the researchers to talk to project staff. This inevitably had some impact on the research timetable, and – considering the distribution of projects – on the timescale of fieldwork.

Table 2.1: A brief description of projects visited for in-depth study

	Project description	Location	Number of clients
1	Organic garden project for people with learning difficulties, mental health problems, a low income and unemployed people	North Midlands	25
2	Organic garden project (with craft workshops) for people with mental health problems and those on low incomes	South East	25
3	Allotment project for people with learning difficulties, mental health problems, a low income and unemployed people	South	50
4	Allotment and outreach project for people with learning difficulties	East Midlands	20
5	Commercial nursery project for people with mental health problems	South	100
6	Garden and workshop project for people with mental health problems, physical and learning disabilities, and those recovering from alcohol and drug addiction	South West Scotland	50
7	Allotment project for people with mental health problems	North Midlands	31
8	Conservation and outreach project for people with learning difficulties	South Wales	10
9	Allotment and garden project for people with learning difficulties and mental health problems	South East	35
10	Community garden and craft workshop for people with learning difficulties	South Wales	20
11	Community learning project for women from black and minority ethnic groups that includes a community garden	North East	4
12	Farm training project for people with learning difficulties and young people with behavioural problems	East Midlands	12
13	Garden and conservation project for people with mental health problems	East Midlands	40
14	Garden project for people with mental health problems and older people	Midlands	70
15	Conservation, woodland, composting and nursery project for people with mental health problems	East Midlands	30
16	City farm with training courses for people with learning difficulties	North	22
17	Outreach and nursery project for people with learning difficulties	North West	18
18	Residential project with garden activities for drug rehabilitation	South West	6
19	Allotment and day centre project for older people, those with physical disabilities and visual impairment	North West	25
20	Allotment project for refugees/people from minority ethnic groups with mental health problems	London	30
21	Allotment project primarily for people with learning difficulties	North	12
22	Garden and workshop training project for unemployed people and those with learning difficulties	London	20
23	Garden project for people with mental health problems, learning difficulties and unemployed	South East Scotland	36
24	Garden project for people with learning difficulties, physical disabilities and mental health problems	South East	160

Access

Successfully gaining access to participants at projects depended on a number of factors:

- the level of reassurance given by the researchers in respect of confidentiality and safe storage of data;
- the degree of vulnerability of the client group concerned – particularly where potential respondents had severe mental health problems, learning difficulties, cognitive or communication impairments;
- managerial concerns relating to ethical procedures, for example. Projects have different mechanisms for 'outsiders' gaining access to clients. Some projects operate on an informal and open basis, while others have more formal procedures that must be recognised and implemented;
- systemic protocols, for example, health and social care ethical research procedures, which must be observed and implemented.

The latter two points are significant in that adherence to ethical criteria, for example, can have serious implications in respect of research procedures. While our study had been approved by Loughborough University's Ethics Committee, research that is conducted on National Health Service (NHS) premises or involves NHS patients or staff must also be approved by a Local Research Ethics Committee (LREC) and, where the research involves more than one NHS domain (the area covered by a Strategic Health Authority), by a Multi-centre Research Ethics Committee (MREC). While these procedures are necessary to protect both agencies and participants involved in research, they can prove time-consuming in respect of the stages and timetabling of research investigations. For example, in order to obtain approval for a study by a LREC or MREC, researchers must submit:

- a completed application form detailing the purpose of the study, the interventions to be examined, the methods to be used and the selection methods for participants;
- a copy of the research proposal and CVs of researchers;
- the letter of invitation to participants;
- consent forms;
- participant information sheets;
- questionnaires, interview protocols and scoring sheets;
- any other documentation relevant to the study.

The preparation of a submission for approval by a REC can be seen, therefore, to be a time-consuming process. Such approval (by an MREC) was necessary in order to carry out telephone interviews with health and social care professionals employed by the NHS.

Confidentiality and consent

Any research study that involves interviewing vulnerable participants should implement effective confidentiality and consent procedures. In our study, both written and verbal assurances were made during initial contact with project staff and before interviews with participants took place in respect of confidentiality. Written consent from participants was also sought. All data in this and all other publications have been anonymised and, as such, all names have been changed or omitted and no contact details are given. All information and data are stored securely and with appropriate reference to the requirements of the 1998 Data Protection Act, for the storage of confidential data.

A key feature of our study has been the use of photographic data. While verbal responses can be anonymised, visual images cannot, and thus the use of photographic images taken on site at projects and of project staff and clients are used in this, and all other publications using data from this study, only with the informed consent of the participants involved. However, as Donaldson (2001, p 4) has recognised: "designing confidentiality and informed consent procedures that take into account photography's loss of privacy will be especially troublesome".

Including vulnerable groups in research can be made more difficult when participants' vulnerabilities mean they do not understand either the terminology, or the concept, of informed consent. When participants have severe learning difficulties, consent procedures require careful consideration. Taking photographs *of* respondents, which include images of people with learning difficulties, and the reproduction of these images for evidential and publication purposes, can prove even more 'troublesome' because respondents in these contexts often do not understand the concept of privacy, confidentiality nor what the consequences for them could be of having their photographs included in a report, for example, which is intended for public record.

In our study, we obtained verbal and written consent to take and use photographs from a number of sources – from project organisers, respondents' advocates and respondents themselves, where possible. However, there remains the problem of enabling those respondents whose cognitive capacities mean they cannot grasp conceptual notions of confidentiality, authority or permission to understand these matters and, more importantly, the consequences of granting permission in the first instance.

Peel (2004) has argued that the issue of consent in research when respondents are vulnerable is rarely straightforward. However, in line with our own institutional ethics procedures and with specific reference to the British Psychological Society Code of Conduct (2004), consent was sought with reference to article 3.6: "Where interventions are offered to those in no position to give valid consent, after consulting with experienced professional colleagues, establish who has legal authority to give consent and seek consent from that person or those persons" (p 3).

A qualitative approach

Five projects were selected for the pilot phase of the study. We aimed to use this phase to trial and, where necessary, modify or adapt the research methodology. Initially it was proposed to use semi-structured interview methods (which would be tape recorded and later transcribed and analysed) and a number of semi-structured questions were devised. Such qualitative research methods place more emphasis on *context and process* (and avoid reliance on pre-ordained tools or instruments). As such, these methods are more appropriate and ideally suited for use among vulnerable respondents, and because priority is given to "the perspectives of those being studied rather than the prior concerns of the researcher" (Bryman, 1989, p 135).

The devised questions observed the themes of social inclusion: social interaction, consumption, production, engagement in the political process and health and well-being. However, following a test interview case (with a mock respondent) prior to interviews with participants at the pilot projects, it was obvious that more vulnerable respondents, for example, those with learning difficulties, may find the 'open-ended' nature of the questions – which allowed for 'departures' and more 'interesting themes to emerge' (see Bryman, 1989) – too difficult to comprehend and respond to. In addition, the number of questions included would be problematic for those with poor concentration or understanding to cope with.

Thus, a more structured approach was utilised, which would *combine methods* of data collection. It was decided that structured questions and a short, taped interview, would only be used among participants who demonstrated that they could answer questions effectively and for reasonably prolonged periods; a shortened, modified set of semi-structured questions would be used among those respondents with learning difficulties or cognitive impairments. Using only semi-structured interview methods among this latter group of respondents would facilitate greater flexibility and would allow the researchers to 'modify the order' in which questions were asked, change the wording of questions and to add or omit 'questions according to their relevance to the particular interviewee' (Arksey, 2004). This technique would thus be more congruent with Burgess's notion of "conversations with a purpose" (1984, p 102).

For those respondents with *severe* learning difficulties or cognitive impairments who could not answer semi-structured interview questions, just four simple questions (which included general questions about gardening and health and well-being outcomes) would be used, tape recorded and later transcribed. Using combined methods would generate statistical data as well as qualitative data useful for 'humanising' the final report. It would also reduce the amount of data and transcription time (which would be manually coded) and would restrict the opportunities for respondents to "take off at a tangent and not cover key areas for the research questions..." (Arksey, 2004, p 271; Measor, 1985). A series of questions was also drawn up for interviews with project organisers, volunteer workers and health and social care practitioners, the latter group being interviewed by telephone.

Outcomes from the pilot study

Adapting the methodology

It became clear that because the study included large numbers of clients affected by mental or physical health problems, cognitive and communication impairments as well as degrees of social exclusion, trying to use one method of data collection to suit all groups would be inappropriate. Once a number of pilot interviews had taken place it was apparent that *depending on the subject group interviewed*, structured and even semi-structured and short interview questions would be inappropriate methods for some respondents. This was especially the case for those respondents with severe learning and communication difficulties.

Thus, where interview techniques would neither be appropriate nor effective, it was initially decided to use observation techniques where researchers would spend time at projects observing activities using standardised themes and notes (and with reference to themes of social inclusion) and attempting to identify case studies of individual respondents where information could be gathered from project 'facilitators' (who knew individual clients well and had monitored their progress over time).

Observation through the use of photographs was also considered to be an important part of the methodology at this stage and would provide appropriate and useful pictorial 'evidence'. This would also be a particularly appropriate method in terms of 'accessible outputs' for vulnerable groups with cognitive or communication difficulties (see Ward, 2004). This does not only apply to those respondents with a cognitive, neurological or physiological impairment but also for those whose common language is not English. Such modification of research methodology is both appropriate and necessary. As Ward has argued (2004, p 171), "Where respondents do not read English, or have difficulty understanding complex information, alternative methodologies must be devised". It is also important to point out here that we use the verbatim quotes of all respondents throughout, but it must be remembered that many respondents did not have equally proficient verbal skills nor did they necessarily use English as their first language.

Ward has further argued that including vulnerable respondents in research processes requires careful preparation (Ward, 2004) and must accommodate the need to include 'facilitators' or arbiters. We successfully used project organisers and other staff as facilitators in our research because, more often, they knew the histories of clients well and were able to provide useful information and advice. Where necessary, they also offered support to clients during and after interviews.

Inclusive or participatory research approaches

However, following a number of interviews and observation periods at the five pilot projects, it became clear that using facilitators and observing and interpreting the activities of clients at projects were not entirely effective research methods in terms of accurately representing the experiences of people with severe learning and communication difficulties. It was agreed that more inclusive, or participatory, techniques might be used more effectively. User-led, participatory or inclusive research methods are not new, but they are generally used among vulnerable groups, such as those with learning difficulties (see Walmsley and Johnson, 2003) and young children.

Photographic participation and elicitation

It is time to reclaim the lost art of using photographs to conduct research and to disseminate results. (Donaldson, 2001)

One of the ways in which we could identify and accommodate more inclusive research approaches, based on the participation of vulnerable respondents, was to use photographic techniques that involved the respondents themselves taking their own photographs in order to further our understanding about their experiences of gardening and horticultural therapy. We decided to give disposable cameras to those participants with severe learning and communication difficulties to use for a period of time during their attendance at gardening projects.

While photo elicitation or elucidation studies have been used in a number of social scientific studies in the past, these terms describe approaches that rely on previously unseen photographic images being used to elicit, or elucidate responses from participants in research. Our approach utilised not only elicitation techniques (whereby participants comment on images they are shown), but also participation methods where participants took the photographs themselves and these were then used to elicit further information; for example, participants were asked to choose a number of 'favourites' and, where possible, expand on their choices.

Our approach meant that not only would we be using photography as a way of illustrating and describing further the types of activities in which all respondents were engaged, and the nature of the horticultural environment in which they worked and socialised, but we would also be enabling those participants with learning difficulties to engage more fully and more *inclusively* in the research process.

In using photographic participation and elicitation techniques we aimed to include particularly vulnerable groups more effectively in the research investigation by identifying a *shared sensory approach* that would accommodate the diversity of participants in our sample and would enable those participants who could not answer questions to describe their experiences in other, more accessible, ways. Photographic participation and elicitation approaches can also prove useful in a number of other ways.

First, they can help overcome the inherent difficulties involved in accurately representing the 'reality' or lived experiences of vulnerable respondents as interpreted through researchers. As Radley and Taylor (2003) have commented, using photographs that have been taken *by* respondents provides "a direct entry into [respondents'] point of view"(p 79). They add:

> **The technique of photography is a culturally fashioned extension of the senses (Lury, 1998) so that it provides a potential 'to question, arouse curiosity, tell in different voices, or see through different eyes from beyond'. (p 79)**

Second, the use of photography can be useful in emphasising the *capacity* of vulnerable respondents rather than their incapacity. It allows us to move away from a pathological medical perspective that narrowly focuses on the deficits of, in this case, people with learning difficulties. The emphasis on pathology here is widely recognised. Lakin (1997), for example, has argued that, "It has been assumed that 'cognitive impairments' – which diagnosticians determine based on performance in vocabulary, memory, math and abstract reasoning – are total impairments, pervasively diminishing everything those so 'afflicted' can do" (p 4).

Third, there are a number of methodological advantages involved in using photographic elicitation approaches. While Donaldson (2001) acknowledges that the tradition of using photographs in research has all but been lost, because researchers choose to adopt methods that 'appear more scientific', it is also true that where photographs have been used in research it has more often been intended as a way of developing research questions rather than to "investigate issues" (Donaldson, 2001, p 1). Although as a research method *on its own* photographic participation and elicitation may be limited in respect of providing evidence, particularly of the kind that may have social and political consequences, used in a flexible or integrative way and as part of a multi-dimensional approach, photographic participation and elicitation may provide important and valuable 'evidence' that other methods may miss.

Donaldson has also further argued, "photographs should not be compared to some hypothetical absolute truth, but only to other data collection methods. In that company, they look pretty good" (2001, p 6). Thus, 'in the company of' statistical data, case studies, the verbatim accounts of respondents themselves and thematic analyses of interviews with reference to the dimensions of social inclusion, photographic participation and elicitation approaches serve not only to add to the methodological rigour of our approach, but also to the appropriate and effective inclusion of specific vulnerable groups in research.

Using photographic participation and elicitation approaches among vulnerable groups focuses on the abilities of, in this case, people with severe learning difficulties, as well as on their 'strong present-orientation' (Booth, 1996). They also provide an opportunity *for those who are able* to be reflective at a later date. As we discuss in the findings (see Chapter 4, p 38) 471 images were generated from this study. Using these images we returned to the projects to ask participants to choose their 'favourites' and to expand on their reasons for their choice. We also conducted a content analysis of these and all the images generated in the photographic participation study. We used the images to elicit further information from those clients who were able to be reflective and to discuss their choices.

Outputs

The output phase of any research study also usually denotes the concluding or end-of-project phase. While publication of this report and its companion guide, *Growing together* (Sempik et al, 2005), represent the concluding stage of our study and are principal elements of its output phase, it is useful to discuss broader points in relation to communication and publication practices here, especially in terms of strategies that have meaning for, and make a difference to, the lives of the people who have participated in the research in the first place.

It is imperative that vulnerable groups are included in research studies. Too often they have been overlooked or purposefully 'left out' of social scientific investigation because of the intention of researchers to 'avoid potential harm' (see Ward, 2004, p 170). And yet it is crucial that research observes the notions of equality of opportunity and social inclusion, particularly in respect of vulnerable groups, in order, as Ward has further argued, "to ensure that the perspectives and experiences of disadvantaged and vulnerable groups are reflected in research findings – and the evidence-based practice which may ensue" (Ward, 2004, p 169).

This latter point is significant in respect of outputs for social action or social policy research in that research findings should influence outcomes for those included in research in the first place and in respect of providing an evidence base for health and social care policy and practice. Thus, research findings must be communicated to as wide an audience as possible and in ways that are appropriate and accessible to the respondent groups and participants in research – in this case, diverse vulnerable and socially excluded groups. In many cases, communicating research findings to wider audiences is influenced by academic agendas and may not always be accessible to those participants without whom there would be no findings to report, particularly when research includes vulnerable respondent groups. Goodley and Moore (2000) have argued:

> **The relationship between the academy and the disability movement is a problematic one. Disability researchers based in the academic world who align themselves with the social model of disability face contradictory aims and values in attempting to challenge dominant modes of research production in ways that signify the importance of the agendas of disabled people. (p 861)**

In many respects, social action research or participatory research, which includes vulnerable groups, must also reconcile the need to be 'credible' with that of being 'useful' (see Walmsley and Johnson, 2003). The promise of our investigation is that any such conflicts are in part reconciled by the advantageous partnership between the academy on the one hand (the research team at Loughborough) and the facilitators and practitioners of STH on the other (the charity Thrive and its members). Findings from this study are thus presented in a number of formats to reach a wide audience of academics, practitioners, policy makers and service users and are also targeted at specific audiences or readers. Thus, this book and its companion volume *Growing together* are two publications among a number of others, including an executive summary of the findings, a dedicated summary for people with learning and communication difficulties, articles in academic and professional journals and results from the photographic participation and elicitation study. The latter will be presented in a visual format with little narrative except to provide a context to the photographs themselves.

The sample of respondents

The clients

One hundred and thirty-seven clients participated in the study (101 male, 36 female). Their ages ranged from 18 to 78 and they represented a number of different vulnerable groups. Table 2.2 summarises this background data. Forty-nine had mental health problems and 43 were able to provide details of their specific diagnoses; this is summarised in Table 2.3. One hundred and seven participants were able to complete a substantial part of the questionnaire.

Table 2.2: Clients taking part in the research

	Male	Female	Total
Mental ill health	37	12	49
Learning difficulties	35	10	45
Physical disabilities/physical illness	4	7	11
Multiple disability	6	1	7
Substance/alcohol misuse	5		5
Vulnerable/unemployed	7	1	8
Minority ethnic group		3	3
Victims of torture	7	2	9
Total	**101**	**36**	**137**
Mean age	42.5	43.1	42.7
SD	14.4	15.0	14.7
Age not known	11	3	14

Note: SD = standard deviation.

Attendance at the project

Length of attendance

Details of the length of attendance at the projects was obtained for 121 clients. The mean period of attendance was 3.4 years (SD = 3.22) and the range varied from one month to 17 years. The remaining 16 clients were unsure of how long they had been attending the project and accurate information could not be provided by project organisers. Two of the clients, however, stated that they had been coming "for a long time". Most clients (76%) had attended a project for more than one year and almost 30% of clients had attended for over three years (this is summarised in Table 2.4). There was little difference in the length of attendance between the two main client groups: clients with mental ill health had attended a project for a mean of 3.1 years ($n = 47$) and clients with learning difficulties 3.6 years ($n = 32$). The difference was not statistically significant ($p>0.05$, t test).

Table 2.3: Clients with mental ill health: self-reported diagnoses

	Number
Anxiety disorders	9
Bipolar disorder	3
Depression	10
Psychosis	3
Post-traumatic stress disorder	2
Schizophrenia	16
No diagnosis	6
Total	**49**

Table 2.4: Clients' duration of attendance at garden projects

Number of years of attendance	Number of clients	%
Less than one year	29	21.2
One to three years	51	37.2
More than three years	41	29.9
Not known	16	11.7
Total	**137**	**100.0**

Frequency and duration of attendance

The mean duration of attendance at a garden project was 5.5 hours (SD = 1.6, n = 125). Some clients engaged in short sessions of no longer than one-and-a-half hours while others spent up to eight hours at the project. Just over half of the clients (50.4%) attended a project for three days of the week or more often.

Referral to projects

More than half of the clients (53%) were referred to a project by a health practitioner or social worker, while almost a third (26.5%) received information informally, 'by word of mouth' and subsequently started at the project. Many of those who provided informal advice and information about projects were members of the Community Mental Health Teams and social workers or fellow patients and colleagues who were attending a garden project. Few, only four clients, started at a project as a result of advertising material distributed by projects.

Project staff, volunteers and health practitioners

Twenty-four project leaders and managers participated in the research in addition to 36 other paid staff. Volunteers, parents and carers, and health and social care professionals who were present at garden projects, were also interviewed. Additionally 11 health practitioners who had experience of garden and horticulture projects participated in semi-structured interviews by telephone and the interviews were recorded. These data are summarised in Tables 2.5 and 2.6.

Table 2.5: Project staff and helpers taking part in the research

Position	Number
Project leaders	24
Other paid staff	36
Volunteers/helpers	14
External professional	9
Parents/carers	5
Total	**88**

Table 2.6: Health professionals taking part in telephone interviews

Position	Number
General practitioners	1
Mental health nurses	5
Psychologists/counsellors	1
Occupational therapists	3
Psychiatric social workers	1
Total	**11**

3 The projects: an overview of garden projects in the UK – structure, management and activities

The research presented in this report has examined the use of *organised* gardening activities for vulnerable people, as opposed to domestic gardening, working under the umbrella of *social and therapeutic horticulture* (STH). This organised form of gardening is centred around horticultural 'projects', which may differ in their specific activities and aims but which have a general common form. They have a clearly defined management and organisation structure with a specific client base for whom fees are usually paid. Information about the structure, management and activities of projects was obtained from a survey of known projects. In 1998 Thrive had carried out a survey of horticulture projects practising STH for vulnerable adults. Around 1,500 projects were identified and became part of a network for the dissemination of information regarding training, meetings and new developments. However, it soon became clear that some of the entries in the database classified as 'projects' were not active ones. Some were individuals with an interest in starting new projects while others were projects that had closed down. In summer 2003 a new survey form was designed and distributed to the 1,500 named individuals within the Thrive network newsletter. Non-respondents were followed up with an additional form and then a telephone call and a total of 836 projects responded to the survey by the end of 2003. The survey provided information about project location, management, client groups and activities. A further 75 projects returned their forms after this time and were not included in the analysis. A total of 911 active projects were thus identified.

The growth of STH projects in the UK

Much has been written about the history of gardening as a therapeutic activity (see Sempik et al, 2003); however, the widespread creation of STH projects in the UK is relatively recent. The first recorded project, which is still active, was founded in 1913 in Ayrshire, Scotland, and four have been active since before 1955. Only 13.2% of projects responding to the survey were started before 1985. From 1986 onwards there was a sharp rise in the number of projects being started that reached its peak in 2002 with 58 new projects in that year. Table 3.1 summarises the number of projects started since 1955.

Although the distribution of projects throughout the UK is not uniform they are to be found in every region (see Table 3.2). The number of projects per 100,000 head of population varies from just below one in Northern Ireland and the North West to almost two per 100,000 in the South West of the UK. It is possible that the apparent scarcity of projects in Northern Ireland is due to the difficulty in identifying and contacting them rather than in an actual low incidence. (Thrive does not have any staff or offices in Ireland and so may have missed active projects in that region.) Indeed, it is possible that the number of projects responding to the survey is an under-estimate of the number of active projects as it is unlikely that all projects responded to the survey. For example, only 29 of the projects

Table 3.1: STH projects started per year

Year	Number of projects started	%
up to 1955	4	0.7
1956-80	30	5.0
1981-85	45	7.5
1986-90	66	11.0
1991-95	112	18.6
1996-2000	209	34.7
2001-	136	22.6
Total	602	100.0
Not known	234	
Total all projects	836	

Note: Percentages of 602 respondents.

Table 3.2: Regional distribution of STH projects in the UK

	Number of projects	%	Regional population (x1,000)	Number of projects per 100,000 head of population
Ireland/Eire	5	0.6	3,917	0.13
Northern Ireland	14	1.8	1,685	0.83
North West	57	7.2	6,729	0.85
London	73	9.2	7,172	1.02
East	56	7.1	5,388	1.04
Yorkshire & the Humber	59	7.4	4,964	1.19
North East	33	4.2	2,515	1.31
East Midlands	56	7.1	4,172	1.34
West Midlands	76	9.6	5,267	1.44
South East	129	16.3	8,000	1.61
Wales/Cymru	48	6.1	2,903	1.65
Scotland	88	11.1	5,062	1.74
South West	98	12.4	4,928	1.99
Total	792	100.0		

Source: UK population figures from the UK 2001 Census; figures for Ireland are taken from the Eire 2002 Census

in the survey were based in prisons or secure psychiatric units. However, recently Grimshaw and King (2003) identified 101 projects within such secure settings, and even this figure may not have revealed the true extent of activity as they only had a 30% response to their survey of prisons and psychiatric units. The survey questionnaires were distributed through the pre-established Thrive network and the survey had been well publicised prior to that, not only through the network but also on the 'Growing Together'[1] website and through practitioners working in the field. A small

---

[1] Information about the study and progress of the research was posted on a dedicated website, which was updated regularly (www.growingtogether.org.uk).

number of projects that had not previously been part of the network also responded. However, it is possible that there are a number of projects still operating outside the network and the true number of active projects is greater than the figure of 911.

Farms and gardens were at one time a feature of many hospitals and some STH projects still have close associations with health trusts – some are managed by them or situated in hospital grounds. There is also a connection with social services departments and other organisations and institutions such as colleges, universities, prisons and so on. This is summarised in Table 3.3. Over half of all projects are associated with or connected to a parent body, organisation or institution. Health trusts and social services have also become involved in starting new projects. While charities were active in starting projects in the beginning, local authorities, the NHS and social services have become involved to a greater extent since the mid-1980s (see Table 3.4).

Type of project sites

STH projects operate on a variety of different sites and some specialise in outreach or contract work and have no garden space of their own. Table 3.5 summarises the different types of project site. 'Gardens' and 'community gardens' make up over half (52%) of the project sites. Almost a fifth of all projects are based on allotments. In many cases allotment plots are leased to STH groups at nominal rents to increase occupancy rates and improve the general appearance of the site.

'Garden' includes walled gardens, vegetable plots, small holdings, hospital and prison gardens and grounds, herb gardens and kitchen gardens.

Table 3.3: Organisations and institutions connected with projects

	Number of projects	%
Hospital	119	14.2
College	99	11.8
Residential home	77	9.2
Community centre	46	5.5
School	39	4.7
Therapeutic community	37	4.4
Rehabilitation centre	36	4.3
Garden centre/commercial	33	3.9
Secure unit	25	3.0
Special school	20	2.4
Hospice	11	1.3
Prison	9	1.1
University	3	0.4

Note: Percentage of 836 respondents.

Table 3.4: Organisations involved in starting projects

Type of organisation	Number of projects started by organisation in year							
	up to 1955	1956-80	1981-85	1986-90	1991-95	1996-2000	2001-	Total
Association/constitution only					1	3	6	10
Charity	2	10	10	18	34	40	29	143
Charity and company ltd by guarantee	2	11	14	17	25	43	25	137
Cooperative				1		2		3
Community group		1			2	6	7	16
Company				1	6	11	10	28
Local authority – social services		3	8	10	11	32	7	71
Local authority – other		1	4	6	8	16	13	48
NHS/health care trust		1	4	8	19	44	29	105
NHS/social services joint		1	4	5	3	10	6	29
No information		1	1		2	2	4	10
Total	**4**	**29**	**45**	**66**	**111**	**209**	**136**	**600**

Table 3.5: Type of project site

	Number of projects	%
Garden	321	38.4
Nursery/garden centre	185	22.1
Allotment	153	18.3
Community garden	117	14.0
Outreach (no one site)	85	10.2
Park/open space/country park	56	6.7
Farm	44	5.3
City farm	20	2.4
Other	16	1.9
Conservation/woodland	15	1.8

Note: Percentage of 836 respondents.

Participation in STH projects

Clients attend projects on a regular basis and projects are available to them on average for four days each week (mean = 4.3, SD = 1.8), although some have limited the attendance of individual clients so that a greater number of clients can participate in activities. Few projects operate a casual or 'drop-in' system and many receive referrals from health trusts and social services departments who pay the client fees. Payment can be on a per capita basis for individual named clients, in the form of a 'block funding' for a specified number of places (although frequently projects take on more clients than the funding covers) or by a direct grant to cover running costs.

Fifty-four projects (of 836 in the survey) were entirely funded by health trusts, 35 entirely by local authorities/social services departments and five by a combination of the two. Around 40% of the total annual budget of all STH projects is provided by health trusts and local authorities.

Many different vulnerable groups participate in STH often working together in the same sessions, and only a minority of projects (35.5%) work with a single group; 64.5% work with two groups or more. The main client groups are those with learning difficulties and mental health needs. However, there are differences in the service provision to these two groups, the costs of that provision and the availability of projects to them. These differences are presented later in this chapter. Tables 3.6 and 3.7 show the number of

Table 3.6: Main client groups using STH projects

	Number of projects	%
Learning difficulties	407	48.7
Mental health needs	339	40.6
Challenging behaviours	144	17.2
Physical disabilities	141	16.9
Unemployed	116	13.9
Multiple disabilities	98	11.7
Young people	91	10.9
Older people	89	10.6
Low income	78	9.3
Drug and alcohol misuse	74	8.9
Rehabilitation	60	7.2
Accident/illness	50	6.0
Visually impaired	45	5.4
Offenders	43	5.1
Hearing impaired	39	4.7
Black and minority ethnic groups	36	4.3
Ex-offenders	31	3.7
Major illness	30	3.6
Homeless and vulnerable housed	20	2.4
Women-only groups	20	2.4
Refugees/asylum seekers	9	1.1

Note: Percentage of all 836 respondents.

Table 3.7: Projects providing a service for single and multiple client groups

Number of client groups	Number of projects	%	Cumulative %
1	234	35.5	35.5
2	120	18.2	53.6
3	95	14.4	68.0
4	78	11.8	79.8
5	54	8.2	88.0
6 or more	79	12.0	100.0

Note: n = 660.

projects providing services to the different client groups and the number of projects working with single and multiple client groups.

The mean number of clients per project was found to be 25.3 (SD = 36.1, n = 609 projects), suggesting that around 21,000 clients use a project each week and that projects provide over one million client sessions (of around 3-6 hours) each year (a summary of the number of clients using STH projects per week is shown in Table 3.8).

The mean number of women using a project was 7.3 (SD = 14.7, n = 587) and six projects had women only as clients. A further 18 projects had over 80% of women as participants. The mean percentage of women as clients at projects was 29% (using a mean project attendance of 25.3 clients per session). The results are summarised in Table 3.9.

Table 3.10 compares the percentage of clients from black and minority ethnic groups at STH projects with the percentage of those minorities in the UK population. African-Caribbean and Black British users made up the two largest single groups of clients from black and minority ethnic groups. The percentage of users from all of the black minority groups (2.93%) was greater than the percentage of those groups in the UK population (2.0%). However, with the exception of Bangladeshi participants, all other groups were under-represented and there appeared to be an under-representation in the total use of STH projects by black and minority ethnic groups.

In most cases, where projects had clients from black and minority ethnic groups, they accounted for only 5% or less of those attending. Only 4.3% of projects recorded that these groups made up 20% or more of their total client numbers. Chinese participants were the least represented minority ethnic group.

Although projects provide many different gardening and horticultural activities, which are discussed at the end of this chapter, these activities are frequently used within the context of specific aims and services, such as training. The most commonly provided services related to social skills development, followed closely by basic skills training and day care/leisure provision (see Table 3.11).

Table 3.8: Clients using the projects per week

Number of clients using the project per week	Number of projects	%
1-10	215	35.3
11-30	258	42.4
31-50	92	15.1
Over 50	44	7.2
Total	**609**	**100.0**

Table 3.9: Women participants at horticultural projects

Percentage of women as participants	Number of projects	%
10% or less	188	32.0
11-30%	182	31.0
31-50%	159	27.1
Over 50%	58	9.9
Total	**587**	**100.0**

Table 3.10: Use of STH projects by black and minority ethnic groups

Minority group	% participation in STH projects[b]	% of UK population (2001 Census)
Mixed race	0.85	1.2
African-Caribbean	1.23	
Black British	1.23	
African	0.47	
Black Caribbean[a]		1.0
Black African[a]		0.8
Black Other[a]		0.2
Indian	0.81	1.8
Bangladeshi	0.68	0.5
Pakistani	0.58	1.3
Other Asian[a]		0.4
Chinese	0.11	0.4
Other races	0.23	0.4
Total: black minority groups	**2.93**	**2.0**
Total: all minority groups	**6.18**	**7.9**

Note: [a] Categories used by National Statistics; population data from UK Census (2001); [b] Calculations based on information from 610 respondents.

Table 3.11: Services provided by projects

	Number of projects	%
Social skills development	378	45.2
Basic skills training	366	43.8
Day care/leisure	365	43.7
Work skills training	321	38.4
Accredited training	215	25.7
Rehabilitation	207	24.8
Sheltered work (unpaid)	165	19.7
Supported employment	95	11.4
Sheltered work (paid)	65	7.8

Note: Percentage of 836 respondents.

Only 25.7% of projects provided accredited training. This was distributed unevenly between the groups. For example, projects for people with learning difficulties provided accredited training more often than those for people with mental health needs (see Table 3.12).

Where major differences exist between service provision for clients with mental health needs and learning difficulties, they are shown in bold in Table 3.12. The results suggest that clients with learning difficulties have greater access to accredited training than those with mental health needs. This is also true with supported employment and work skills training.

Table 3.12: A comparison of services and opportunities provided to clients with mental health needs and to those with learning difficulties

	Mental health needs[a] (*n* = 180)	% (of 180)	Learning difficulties[b] (*n* = 201)	% (of 201)
Accredited training	26	14.4	96	38.7
Basic skills training	83	46.1	148	59.7
Day care/leisure	107	59.4	132	53.2
Rehabilitation	94	52.2	20	8.1
Sheltered work (paid)	17	9.4	24	9.7
Sheltered work (unpaid)	33	18.3	75	30.2
Social skills development	106	58.9	137	55.2
Supported employment	14	7.8	44	17.7
Work skills training	66	36.7	135	54.4

Notes: [a] The projects included in column 2 provide services for clients with mental health and other needs but not for those with learning difficulties.

[b] Similarly the projects included in column 4 provide services for clients with learning difficulties but not mental health needs.

Rehabilitation is offered to more clients with mental health needs than those with learning difficulties. However, a standardised definition of 'rehabilitation' was not used in the questionnaire and it may be that services provided to clients who have a condition or illness from which they may recover, such as mental health problems, are viewed collectively as 'rehabilitation'. The term 'rehabilitation', therefore, is unlikely to be used to describe services offered to people with learning difficulties, unless they also have additional problems of illness or are recovering from injury.

Staffing and volunteers

Over 80% of projects operated with some full-time paid staff. The mean number of full-time paid staff at a project was 2.2 (SD = 2.8, *n* = 541). More than half of the projects (51.8%) had one or two full-time paid members of staff, similarly, most projects (53.5%) employed one or two part-time staff. However, 19.5% of all projects had no full-time paid staff and 31 (3.7%) projects reported that they had no paid staff at all. Seventy-three projects (13.4%) employed part-time paid staff but had no full-time members and over 70% of projects used unpaid volunteers to assist them (see Tables 3.13-3.15).

Qualifications of project staff

The qualifications of project staff are shown in Table 3.16. Almost 40% of projects had staff with formal qualifications in horticulture but only 10.2% had qualifications in therapeutic horticulture (or horticultural therapy). This is not particularly surprising since the availability of training in therapeutic

Table 3.13: Number of full-time paid staff at STH projects

Number of full-time staff	Number of projects	%
0	106	19.5
1	166	30.6
2	115	21.2
3	54	9.9
4	37	6.8
5	24	4.4
6-10	26	4.8
More than 10	15	2.8

Note: n = 543.

Table 3.14: Number of part-time paid staff at STH projects

Number of part-time staff	Number of projects	%
0	130	25.0
1	170	32.6
2	109	20.9
3	33	6.3
4	30	5.8
5	16	3.1
6-10	27	5.1
More than 10	6	1.2

Note: n = 542.

Table 3.15: Number of regular volunteers or helpers at STH

Number of volunteers/ helpers	Number of projects	%
0	145	29.4
1	91	18.4
2	67	13.6
3	40	8.1
4	24	4.9
5	29	5.9
6-10	56	11.3
More than 10	42	8.5

Note: n = 494.

Table 3.16: Formal qualifications of project staff

Qualification	Number of projects	%
Horticulture	333	39.8
Health and social care	231	27.6
Teaching	221	26.4
Horticultural therapy	85	10.2
Occupational therapy	40	4.8
Nursing	22	2.6

Note: n = 836.

horticulture in the UK is limited. A small percentage (4.8%) of projects had staff with qualifications in occupational therapy. This does, however, represent 40 individual projects.

Financial management of STH projects

Total running costs of projects

A total of 590 projects supplied some estimates of their total annual running costs. A total of 37.6% operated on a budget of less than £10,000 and 71.7% of all projects had a budget of less than £50,000 (see Table 3.17). Not surprisingly, those with larger budgets were able to support more clients but the relationship between the size of budgets and the

Table 3.17: Project costs and number of clients at the project

Total annual budget	Mean number of clients	Number of projects
Less than £10,000	15.1	200
£10,000-£50,000	26.6	187
£50,000-£100,000	32.6	84
£100,000-£500,000	41.5	72
Over £500,000	50.0	3

Note: Data from 546 projects.

number of clients was not linear. Projects with large budgets supported disproportionately fewer clients than those with smaller ones.

Estimating the total cost of the project network and the cost of an individual client session

In order to estimate the total annual cost of all of the projects the midpoint of each range was taken to be the annual cost of that project (except in the case of the four projects with the highest costs where a value of £500,000 was used).

The sum of costs for 590 projects was found to be £38,465,000 and extrapolating this to the whole network of 836 projects produced a value of £54,502,949. Assuming that projects provided 1,015,248 sessions annually, as previously estimated, the mean cost of an individual session was £53.68.

Project costs and client group

The project costs varied according to the main client group at the project. For example, project costs were greater for those projects that provided a service for clients with learning difficulties than for those that provided a service for people with mental health problems. Table 3.18 summarises the costs of projects that cater for only one of those two groups (that is, those

Table 3.18: A comparison of total annual costs of projects for people with learning difficulties and those with mental health problems

Total annual cost	Learning difficulties[a]	%	Mental health needs[b]	%
Less than £10,000	60	27.4	93	58.1
£10,000-£50,000	85	38.8	39	24.4
£50,000-£100,000	39	17.8	15	9.4
£100,000- £500,000	33	15.1	13	8.1
Over £500,000	2	0.9	0	0
Total	**219**	**100.0**	**160**	**100.0**

Notes: [a] Excluding mental health needs. [b] Excluding learning difficulties. Projects may include other client groups.

projects that take clients with learning difficulties *and* those with mental health problems are excluded from the analysis). More projects for clients with mental health needs fall into the lowest cost category than those for clients with learning difficulties. Similarly, more projects for clients with learning difficulties fall into the higher cost categories.

The information supplied by the projects was used to calculate the individual cost of a client session for the projects in Table 3.18. The cost of a session for clients with learning difficulties was calculated to be £63.45 and £34.69 for those with mental health needs. If the same calculation was carried out for those projects that only take a single client group, the estimates were £56.57 and £38.92 respectively. This difference could be due to higher staffing levels at projects for people with learning difficulties mentioned previously. The mean number of staff at projects that provide a service only for clients with mental health needs (that is, and accept no other client groups) was 1.6 (SD = 1.3, n = 68) while at those projects only for people with learning difficulties it was 2.5 (SD = 3.4, n = 101). However, this difference was not statistically significant ($p>0.05$, Mann-Whitney U test). The number of clients at the projects was similar, with a mean of 22.5 (SD = 45.5, n = 66) at projects for people with mental health needs and 23.2 (SD = 18.7, n = 97) at those for clients with learning difficulties.

Projects for people with learning difficulties were also available to their clients more often than those for people with mental health problems (see Table 3.19), and this may also contribute to the differences in costs.

Interestingly, the published costs of day centre attendance also show a similar difference between client groups. Day care provided by local authorities social services costs around £36 per day for people with mental health problems and £54 for people with learning difficulties (see Netten et al, 2001, pp 57, 58, 73, 74).

Table 3.19: Mean number of days that projects are open per week

	n	Days project open
Projects that have clients with mental health needs but not learning difficulties	165	3.58
Projects that have clients with learning difficulties but not mental health needs	235	4.49
Projects that only have clients with mental health needs (single client group)	85	3.52
Projects that only have clients with learning difficulties (single client group)	109	4.34
All projects	**614**	**4.26**

Client fees

Where a charge was made for clients the mean client fee per session was £27.06; however, only 120 provided details of the fee charged, a further 43 reported that the charge was zero. Table 3.20 summarises the client fees charged by projects.

Table 3.20: Client fees charged per session

	Number of projects	%
No charge	43	26.4
£10 or less	17	10.4
Over £10-£30	66	40.5
Over £30-£50	30	18.4
Over £50	7	4.3

Note: Percentage of 163 respondents.

Sources of project funding

Only 38.2% of projects were funded by a single source of income. Most projects (85.4%) relied on up to three main sources of funding. Table 3.21 shows the numbers of projects receiving funding from the various sources and the percentage of their income from those sources. The final

Table 3.21: Main sources of project income

Source of funding	Number of projects	Estimated % of project's annual budget from funding source (mean)	% of TOTAL budget for ALL projects
Central government	85	10.3	10.2
Charitable trusts	146	8.9	6.4
Client fees – direct payment by clients	50	1.4	1.2
Client fees – paid by local authorities/social services	151	14.7	18.8
Client fees – paid by health trusts	28	1.4	1.0
Client fees – combined health and social services	31	2.9	3.8
National Lottery	50	3.9	2.3
Corporate	19	0.3	0.3
European sources	63	3.4	6.0
Health trusts (other than client fees)	131	17.1	10.6
Learning and Skills Councils	75	6.6	7.3
Local government (other than client fees)	106	10.9	10.9
Public fundraising	83	2.6	1.3
Self-generated sales	220	9.6	17.1
Unable to answer	43		
Other sources	44	10.3	3.0

Note: Total number of respondents = 578.

column shows the percentage of income from the different sources of the total combined budget of all projects (that is, the percentage of the total amount of money expended by the sources on the projects in the survey)[2]. Client fees, paid by local authorities, social services and health trusts, accounted for 23.6% of the total annual budget, and payments (other than client fees) by them amounted to 21.5% of the costs. Therefore, almost half of the costs of STH projects are borne by local authorities and health trusts. A significant income was received from commercial activities (17.1%), but very little from fundraising or from corporate sponsorship. Similarly, there was little income from fees paid directly by clients.

Gardening activities

STH projects provide a variety of activities for their clients and while many of those can be described as 'horticulture' because they involve plant care and propagation, others can be viewed as 'garden' activities because they take place in and around the garden or serve to enhance the aesthetic appeal of the garden or its access or maintenance. Indeed, the construction, decoration and maintenance of a garden involves many different tasks – landscaping, building, art and crafts – in addition to planting and plant care. Other activities have developed as a result of clients' needs, for example, literacy or numeracy training, or because of client interests or wishes, or as a result of the expertise of project staff. These activities can be classified broadly as follows:

- horticultural activities – activities involving plants and a knowledge of plant care (or carried out under supervision), for example, sowing seeds, pricking out seedlings, planting plants, greenhouse work, preparing beds for planting;
- landscaping activities – preparing general garden schemes, laying paths and slabs, preparing new beds;
- building and construction – constructing items specifically for the garden – sheds, outhouses, stone and brickwork;
- garden craft – producing mainly small items that can be used in the project garden or sold for use in other gardens, for example, garden seats, bird and bat boxes, sundials, gates and railings;
- garden art – producing purely decorative items for the garden project (or for sale), for example, garden statues and murals;
- rural crafts – preparing items that are not necessarily for garden use but where the process of production or the artefacts themselves have a traditional link with gardens or the 'outside environment' or are assembled from it, for example, wood turning in the open air using a pole lathe, firing pottery in an open air turf kiln or making charcoal from wood gathered from the project site;

[2] The value of each source of income was calculated for every project and summated to provide the total contribution for that source. The percentages in column 4 of Table 3.21 were adjusted so that the total was 100%.

- arts and crafts not related to gardens – art and craft work that has no specific link to horticulture and gardening but which is carried out in workshops associated with the STH project, for example, painting, pottery and mosaics. Almost 20% of STH projects have an arts or crafts workshop;
- offsite work – gardening or conservation work carried out away from the project site. This includes garden maintenance, construction and care of footpaths, stiles and general conservation work, collection of material for composting. Although many projects are involved in outreach work, 10% of projects are engaged solely in such work and have no project sites or gardens of their own;
- formal training programmes in horticulture and gardening, for example, NPTC or NVQ accredited training in land-based subjects;
- basic skills training including literacy, numeracy, information technology and general life skills such as food preparation and cookery. Forty-four per cent of projects that responded to the survey provided such training;
- commercial activities and the formation of commercial units, including social firms and cooperatives. Around 17% of the total budget of STH projects is derived form sales and services.

These activities make up STH; they serve to establish and improve the garden or project space and improve the skills and knowledge of participants and may also provide formal qualifications. Proceeds from artefacts and produce sold by the projects, and services provided by them, supplement the project income. The project site, therefore, acts as a physical and organisational hub of the processes; it is where the participants gather to work in the space itself, or meet to go off to other workshops or outreach work. The space is improved and decorated by their activities and the artefacts that they produce. Some participants will try their hand at many or all of these activities while others will limit themselves to specific ones (some are limited by their disabilities). Those working on tasks that do not involve planting or 'horticulture' in its strictest sense still consider themselves as 'gardeners' because of their association with the project as a whole and with the garden itself.

Project organisers encourage clients and volunteers to participate in as many activities as possible and frequently clients suggest ideas for new ones, for example, a hide to observe birds around a wildlife pond was built at one project on the instigation of the clients. Interest in blacksmithery at another project led to the building of a forge and the employment of a resident blacksmith to instruct clients and volunteers.

The construction and landscaping of a garden also produced a change in the natural environment. For example, many of the gardens were created on derelict land such as abandoned allotment plots and project organisers were keen to show photographs of the development of their project sites. Such large-scale change is exciting and interesting for all participants. Yet it would seem that such change only occurs at the beginning of a project's life and that once it is established the tasks are limited to garden maintenance and annual planting. Although these may be interesting and satisfying in themselves, and form the basis of much of what we understand as traditional gardening, the scope of activities for clients could be curtailed. Many of the projects that we visited, therefore, engaged in 'mini-projects', that is, small-scale landscaping exercises to prepare specific garden features or small 'show gardens' similar to those seen at major horticultural shows. For example, two of the projects had independently constructed 'beach gardens' complete with sand, shingle, deckchairs and assorted flotsam. A number of the projects had wildlife gardens with ponds and areas of wetland. One had built a Zen garden with sunken rocks and white gravel. A greater availability of land allowed one project to plant a five-acre vineyard. The small-scale designs are reversible and the land can be used for other purposes when required. Frequently, these new ventures were able to attract funding from organisations that were unable (or unwilling) to fund the ongoing or core costs of an STH project.

STH is not a specific entity that can be regarded as a single intervention but a collection of activities that frequently involves people with different vulnerabilities and disabilities (and those with none) working together in the garden space (or in activities associated with it or connected to it). It is distinct from 'horticultural therapy', a term that is used more often in the US than the UK, and that is defined by UK practitioners as:

> **... the use of plants by a trained professional as a medium through which certain clinically defined goals may be met. (Growth Point, 1999, p 4)**

While 'therapeutic horticulture' is defined as:

> **... the process by which individuals may develop well-being using plants and horticulture. This is achieved by active or passive involvement. (Growth Point, 1999, p 4)**

Horticulture in this definition is used in its broadest sense and includes activities and processes that are found in and around the gardens and sites of STH projects. The term 'social and therapeutic horticulture', which is used by Thrive and by practitioners in the UK, acknowledges the social dimensions of those activities, that is, that the benefit is not solely reliant on the interaction between the practitioner and the client but on the interaction between all participants – clients, staff and volunteers.

4 The findings

Introduction to themes from the interviews

Interview transcripts were analysed thematically. Broad themes and sub-themes were identified from an initial reading of the transcripts and new themes and sub-themes were added to the list as they were observed. Sections of the transcripts pertaining to those themes were stored in a specially constructed database and were assigned a descriptor. All sections relevant to a specific theme or sub-theme could then be viewed together. The themes identified from client interviews are shown in Table 4.1.

Many of the themes that appeared in the transcripts of clients were also present in those of project staff. The context of those themes was also at times the same. For example, both clients and project staff spoke of their enjoyment of working outside in the fresh air and in the natural surroundings, and of seeing plants grow. However, some themes were specific to the transcripts of staff and these are presented in Table 4.2. These deal with the activities and aims of the projects and a general reflection on the principles of STH and the philosophy and ethos of organic approaches.

Table 4.1: Themes emerging from interviews with STH project clients

Main theme	Sub-themes	Additional sub-themes
Nature	Being outside; fresh air; seeing things grow; aesthetic; sensory; seasons; weather; connectedness with nature	Witnessing the entire growing process; fascination
Nurture	Looking after; cultivation; food	Feeling useful; satisfaction
Social	Mixing; making friends; belonging; working together; sharing problems; staff support	Cooperation; like-minded; common purpose
Space	Sanctuary; safety; improvement; creation; care; belonging	
Physical	Exercise; stamina; energy; physical improvement	
Mental	Experience of health services; medication; mood	
Mood	Peacefulness; relaxation; enjoyment; humour; distraction; reflection; memories; escape	
Well-being	Self-confidence; self-esteem; independence	
Work	Status; pay; lack of pressure; enjoyment; productivity; variety; off-site work; machinery and tools; structure; teamwork; social; finding employment	Risk and dangers from machinery and tools
Economic	Project income; stake	
Education	Learning; knowledge; qualifications	Learning and training in gardening, machinery, organic methods
Environment	Organic; avoiding chemicals; protecting the environment; health; food	
Creativity	Art; craft; construction	
Spiritual	Earth; healing	Nature

Table 4.2: Additional themes from interviews with project staff

Main theme	Sub-themes
Project	Aims; activities
Social	Integration; inclusion; acceptance; sense of identity; becoming communicative
Space	Sense of place; culture; ownership
Mood	Concentration
Work	Welfare benefits; choice
Economic	Project income; stake
Education	Evidence; assessment; assistance; progression; learning from clients
Environment	Organic philosophy; biodynamic gardening; sustainability

The themes from the interviews, and observations at the projects, were used to identify a number of broader areas of interest arising from STH projects. These are as follows and are dealt with in turn in subsequent sections of this chapter:

- nature, freedom, and space;
- the social dimension of gardening projects;
- issues relating to work and employment;
- physical activity, health and well-being;
- development of self-confidence and self-esteem;
- the involvement of vulnerable clients in the research process;
- garden projects and environmental philosophies.

Distinguishing between clients and volunteers

Throughout this report we have used the term 'client' to refer to the intended beneficiary of a garden project for whom a fee is usually paid, either by a health trust (or other care agency) or by the client him/herself. We have referred to project staff as 'organisers' or 'workers'. While a clear distinction can be made between paid project staff and fee-paying clients, the distinction, with regard to support needs, between unpaid helpers or volunteers and clients is often not so clear. Some people volunteer to help with garden projects simply because they have time on their hands (some have retired, for example), they have a keen interest in gardening and horticulture, and in some cases they also wish to help the local community. These volunteers have little or no emotional or physical support needs. However, others who volunteer may deliberately be seeking an environment, activity or company that they perceive to be helpful or even 'therapeutic' in their particular circumstances. Frequently, these people have mental health needs or have suffered (often severe) emotional traumas such as bereavement, divorce or redundancy and consequently have emotional needs. They may be lacking in self-esteem and self-confidence, for example, due to long-term unemployment. It is not clear why some of these volunteers do not attend as clients. It is possible that they may be outside of the groups that are funded by local health trusts and social care agencies or outside of the usual profile of those seeking care. For example, long-term unemployed people may not see themselves as needing care but may be looking for a 'worthwhile' activity to fill their spare time.

The following short case history illustrates the way in which a garden project can provide support for one of its volunteers:

Case history: Cathy

Cathy had been made redundant some time previously and was looking for a new direction. She had an interest in horticulture so decided to pursue that avenue:

> "I was made redundant about four years ago and I wanted to do something for me as well as pursuing my career goals and I was looking for a change of direction and horticulture was what I wanted to do really because it's been a leisure pursuit all my life and I decided maybe it was time to put some time and energy into going that sort of direction."

She obtained part-time work as a gardener and after about a year started attending an organic garden project as a volunteer. The project provides a service for people with learning difficulties for which it receives pay, and also uses many volunteers to help maintain the organic garden. It is well known in the local area and Cathy was attracted to it by the organic methods and a shared interest in sustainable practices.

Although it seemed at first during the interview that redundancy had provided Cathy with a welcome opportunity for a career change, it became clear that the process had been deeply traumatic and that she perceived her present work as a gardener to have been beneficial to her health and well-being at a difficult time in her life:

> "... but overall the benefits [of her job as a part-time gardener] and certainly to me the health benefits to me have been quite significant over the time."

> "... because of the, well because of how I reacted to my redundancy. I'd been working for 25 years as a [...], I was doing something that I really loved and I thought I was very good at and I took that experience very, very badly and I'm still recovering from it."

The garden project appeared to be the environment that she had been searching for and in which she felt comfortable. It provided her with a social dimension that she perceived as important, and also the opportunity to help other clients. The helping and caring aspect was also significant as her employment prior to redundancy had involved career counselling – an aspect of her professional role which she both enjoyed and at which she considered herself to be good.

> "Yes, I think after several years of trying different things and looking for different things I feel very comfortable here, I wasn't actually feeling too well this morning but I was really looking forward to coming here and to some extent that probably made the difference between whether I did come along or not, I wanted to be here and I do enjoy being here with the people, the organisers take a real interest in what you want to do but also what you're capable of doing."

> "I personally need the contact with other people as I'm much better at solving things or sorting things out by talking things through with other people and sometimes if I've got too long to think about things on my own I can actually become quite negative."

> "I feel a real privilege but I feel it's going to be something that once I get on top of I'm going to have quite a lot of other experiences that I can then share with other people and I think that's quite a need that I had, not to just do it for my own personal use but to encourage other people to get involved is something I do feel quite passionate about, and I feel that this sort of environment is going to hopefully bring that out in me. I've been a bit lame in the last few years as I've been struggling to, you know, make sense of a lot of things and a lot of losses in my life and so this feels as though I'm moving forward."

The project provided Cathy with many of the same benefits as it did for the clients, for example, the prospect of working in a peaceful, natural environment, an activity that had some similarities to paid employment but which lacked the pressure, the opportunity for social interaction and the opportunity to learn new skills. It also returned to her certain roles which she had enjoyed in her previous, professional role and which she had lost as a result of redundancy. These dimensions led to an increased self-confidence and self-esteem, a process which was aided by the care and interest of the project staff.

The support needs of many volunteers were recognised by project organisers and projects appeared willing to accept volunteers with such needs. The 'open door' approach of some of the projects allowed this to occur. However, some project workers did express concern about the problems and risks posed by such volunteers as their medical and social histories were unknown. This was in contrast to 'formal' clients whose backgrounds and medical histories were known to the referring agencies and which were passed to project workers. While some carried out checks on volunteers with the Criminal Records Bureau, others considered such a practice too intrusive and opted instead to "keep a close eye" on new volunteers and limit or supervise their contact with clients. Indeed, some project workers did not enquire about the backgrounds of volunteers or keep formal records about them, considering also that that was intrusive, and preferred instead to find out their histories by informal chats and conversation. The time taken up by such volunteers was probably not great and did not interfere with the support given to clients. Volunteers were able to provide labour and expertise and so assist the project and were responsible for few, if any, additional costs to the project.

Some clients continued to work at their project as volunteers after their formal (paid-for) period of attendance had ended. Such arrangements were generally encouraged and facilitated where possible (by finding funds if needed). In a number of instances clients stayed on to become volunteers, then were employed in a part-time or casual capacity, before becoming full-time, paid members of staff. Such progression was not unusual and cases were observed at five of the projects visited. Additionally, project workers described other instances where this had occurred. During their time as volunteers, and also during their time as employees, these people received support from the project staff and also the benefits attributable to the activities and environment of the project (see Case history: Cathy, page 40).

The terminology used at projects may also help to blur the distinction between clients and volunteers. The term 'volunteer' is used by some projects as a term for their clients (to avoid the stigmatisation of the individual with a 'medical' term such as 'client' or 'service user'), while other projects only use the term to describe an unpaid helper. Some projects did not make a distinction between their clients and their volunteers or helpers and all were referred to as 'project members', volunteers or even 'gardeners'. In some cases this was part of a deliberate policy to integrate all participants of the project, including staff, clients and volunteers and make no distinction between them. Other projects differentiated between clients and helpers by the terms they used, but acknowledged that the boundary between the two groups was indistinct, as the example below shows:

> **"And they said, 'We don't like being called clients. We're coming here as volunteers, of our own free will, we don't have to come here if we don't want to. So, we're volunteers, please'. And so we've always called them volunteers since, so therefore any volunteers/helpers that came to help had to be called 'friends', really, because we don't confuse the two, although the borders**

are very.... I mean, most of the people who come in as friends actually really could qualify as volunteers and some people who come as volunteers feel that they could just be helpers really ... there isn't much borderline between the two, really." (Ann, project organiser, project for people with mental ill health)

All of the projects visited had an organised management structure, paid staff and an identifiable client group (although some deliberately chose to call them by other names). Some also had volunteers drawn from vulnerable groups, most frequently people with mental health problems or those with emotional needs. However, it is known that other projects operate a less formal policy, without clients who are referred by care agencies or trusts but with participants, who as volunteers, choose to engage in the project activities. Some of those participants also have support needs, and these are met by the group as a whole (in an informal way). The participants in such a type of project probably receive similar (if not the same) benefits as the clients who attend more structured and organised projects, such as those observed in this research. What differentiates these groups of projects is their organisational structure or management processes, and what appears to distinguish clients from volunteers is not necessarily their individual needs but rather, whether fees have been paid specifically on their behalf.

Nature, freedom and space

One of the defining features of STH is that most of the activities take place outdoors in a 'natural' environment. Although the garden sites are cultivated and managed, they are 'natural' inasmuch that they have access to plants, trees, wildlife and are open to the sky and the weather. Consequently, themes related to *nature*, *being outside* and *in the fresh air* were frequently expressed by both clients and project workers during interviews.

Many projects also provided indoor or sheltered activities associated with horticulture and gardening, for example, in greenhouses and polytunnels (as distinct from indoor craft activities) and frequently these were not distinguished from the outdoor ones by the clients. Clients still considered themselves to be 'outside' even when they were in a greenhouse or shed. It became clear that 'being outside' had different meanings to different people and that different people may have had different purposes in seeking to go 'outside'. A number of separate components appear to be involved in the respondents' perception and enjoyment of being 'outside'. These included a desire to *escape*, to be away from the constraints and demands of the 'inside' which could be a workplace, institution or their own home; the desire to be in contact with elements of the *natural environment* including plants, changing seasons and weather; a feeling of *'connectedness' with nature* and an understanding of their place in the greater natural world; a fascination with being able to see the *process of growth* and being able to assist and nurture it; a wish for a peaceful or *tranquil setting* with a slower pace of life; the opportunity to 'improve' or change a project garden or site (frequently by 'working together' with nature) and *a sense of place* – that is, an emotional attachment to the physical space of the project garden. Additionally the outside environment was seen as a democratising factor by project workers – where clients and staff could work together on an equal basis and learn from each other.

Escape

'Being outside' was used by some clients as an expression of escape from the confinement of the physical indoor environment and its associated equipment, such as computers and television. When they spoke of their enjoyment of being outside they frequently made the comparison with the factory or the office, as the following two quotes illustrate:

> "Um, being outside is very nice, enjoyable, I mean I've had jobs and I've worked in factories and stuff before now and it's just nice to be in the open, be a bit like free." (Peter, project client with mental ill health)

> "I don't know whether I could actually say specifically. It's just in my nature to want to be outside and be practical. And, I mean, I can't stand being in an office or with, sort of, computers, I don't even like watching television. I like to be out in the fresh air in all weathers." (Tony, project client with mental ill health)

The escape could also be from the restraining or inhibiting consequences of an illness and not solely from a physical environment. The reference to the 'inside' in the following quote can be seen as a metaphor for the limitations caused by the client's illness:

> "Oh, I just like being out in the fresh air, it just seems natural, you know. I mean, my life has been, really inside and, really, sort of, closed off for a long time, you know, because of my illness." (Dave, project client with mental ill health)

The notion of escape is not only the process of getting away from the undesirable features of the indoor environment but also that of moving into a preferred space. Such a concept has been used by Kaplan and Kaplan (1989) who proposed that the natural environment has a 'restorative' effect on directed attention that has become fatigued (attention restoration theory). One component of the restorative environment, they suggested, is *being away*, which:

> ... implies involving oneself in cognitive content different from the usual. For large numbers of individuals in the developed countries, nature is no longer the usual everyday content. As

such nature meets this criterion with little difficulty. That is not to say that, for a given individual, there are not many other forms of being away. (Kaplan and Kaplan, 1989, p 189)

Being away, they proposed, was not simply 'escape' but had the added dimension of movement into another world, which had 'coherence' and 'extent'. In other words the new world contained elements that were interrelated and part of a perceived greater system or process (see Kaplan and Kaplan, 1989, pp 183-4). The clients in our study also wished to escape into a natural surrounding in which they were not only outside but where their environment was calm and peaceful and included elements of nature. The peacefulness of the natural space was frequently compared with the noisiness of the built environment, even if that was also an outdoor environment. Escape, therefore, could be from an unfavoured outdoor place, such as a busy city, into the favoured outdoor natural environment:

> **"Well, outside in nature, sure, but I mean, outside in the traffic, you know, it doesn't do much for me, really. But, you know, to be surrounded by green trees, grass, flowers, and birds twittering, and yeah, I like it." (John, project client with mental ill health)**

> **"Well, I find it really peaceful, actually. It's nice to be out in the country. Erm, there's loads of wildlife around. It's just nice just to see nature takes its course, you know? Because compared to Bristol, well, that was just like a concrete jungle. So it's nice to be out in the fields, and that, and, yeah, it's very, sort of, calming in a way." (Robert, project client with mental ill health)**

In addition to the peaceful qualities of the environment there was a perception by many clients and project staff that being in the 'fresh air' was healthy and comparisons were made with the unhealthy atmosphere of the city. The outdoor environment was seen as synonymous with physical exercise and energy:

> **"It's just working outdoors, really, that I enjoy.**

> **"Well, it's a healthy occupation, you know, because you're getting a lot of oxygen from the plants." (Steve, project client with multiple disabilities)**

> **"The being outside, the fresh air, the exercise, it's exhilarating, it gives you energy. Your energy increases as you work.... Well it's out in the country which means lots of fresh air as opposed to being in the city. And working outdoors and it's a good setting, like on a day like today where there's snow on the ground and the sun, and the people are good, there's a good crowd." (Sheila, project client with mental ill health)**

For some clients the sense of 'being outside' also extended to the enclosed structures of the garden. They felt 'outside' even when they were working in the greenhouse or polytunnel. Perhaps the transparency of these structures allowed them to be a part of the 'outside' because it was clearly visible to them, or perhaps their lightweight physical construction differentiated them from 'buildings' or structures of the built environment. It is also possible that such structures are a part of the construct of 'garden' and hence are associated with the outside. They are also distinct from buildings, for example, because they carry none of the demands or imperatives associated with factories, offices, homes or institutions. Escaping to the garden shed or greenhouse, therefore, may be seen as no different to escaping to the garden itself. It is interesting that in the study of open spaces, researchers also need to define what they mean as 'outside'. For example, Ward Thompson (2004, p 1), in her study of the use of outdoor environments, included all those that were "open to the sky, from urban streets and courtyards to remote rural hilltops". However, such a definition may not include all of the spaces that are considered by users of garden projects to be part of the outside environment. Indeed, to them, sheds and the like may be 'covered' or sheltered parts of the outside.

The aesthetic value of the natural environment

The natural environment provides many elements that the clients found pleasurable and interesting and which captured their attention. They were keen to recount their experiences of the sounds and sensations of their environment, for example:

> "I find that I have moments when, especially here, because there's so much nature around. I mean, there's the trees. You might just, yeah, just watch the wind blowing through the leaves, or watch a bird on a branch, or there's a stream down the bottom. Listen to that gurgling along when it just goes on and on and on, it's never-ending." (Andrew, project client with history of substance misuse)

Some of the clients expressed their emotions regarding the appearance or smell of the plants and flowers in the garden and recalled childhood memories of the plants and flowers:

> "Well, I like working in the open air, anyway. And, as I say, it gives me pleasure to watch things that I've planted, and watching them grow, and, you know, when I, because I haven't been here much since Christmas, when I went round to my scented garden, I was so pleased because it still looked lovely, you know, the flowers were still out and it still looked nice." (Paula, project client with physical disabilities)

"I remember I had an awful thing about flowers when I was a wee boy, which is one of my most fetish, for flowers, because of the smell of them, the perfume ... I like the rhododendrons, I remember I liked them. And all the tulips and the daffodils. And I had a thing about hyacinths, I liked all the patterns on them.

"... I liked all the [...] I'm not too keen on certain plants because some of them don't look [...] and they smell [...]. I don't like the laburnum, that's a bit too poisonous.... But I like certain plants that have a perfumed smell like rosehip, lavender, plants like that, you know, that do have a textured smell, it's the nature of the plants in Scotland." (Alan, project client with mental ill health)

There was also a desire to observe the whole natural process of growth, from the sowing of a seed to the harvesting of the fruit, and to participate in that process by tending plants and caring for them. Thus nurturing or 'looking after' plants and seedlings made clients feel useful and needed:

"It's nature. You see progress with the plants at the end of [...]. The plants need you, really. If you just let them grow wild, they need you to look after them, you feel useful." (Elaine, project client with mental ill health)

Being a witness to the whole growing process also provided a sense of fascination, especially if the final product could be eaten:

"I think it's just, like, to see it progress, really. You know, starting off with, like, a bag, you know, a packet of seeds, and, seeing the end results and having the end results on the table, usually to eat [laughs].

"But it's nice to see it because, you know, because nature's an amazing thing, isn't it? And just to see something start from seed and then grow into a, you know, something you can eat, is quite amazing." (Robert, project client, long-term unemployed)

Cultivation of food was particularly important to some clients (and project workers), particularly those who took an interest in organic gardening. This was seen as an alternative to the chemically contaminated produce sold in supermarkets and provided project participants with a sense of control. They knew what went into the production of their crops, which was not the case with commercially produced ones. Many clients and project workers also had wider environmental interests and expressed strong views in that direction. Of the projects visited, most did not use chemical fertilisers and pesticides, choosing instead to use organic methods. The influence of environmental views and philosophies on project activities is discussed in detail on page 111.

The notion of nurture as an important process in project activities was recognised by the staff and used in the teaching of life skills. For example, clients took responsibility for the care of plants; if those plants were neglected they did not survive. In this way horticulture was used to demonstrate the needs of other living things. It also showed that outputs, such as a healthy, abundant crop, were dependent on the care and nurture provided by the clients:

> "I think one of the biggest things about a garden is the very fact that it is alive, and it responds to whatever you do. And people can see the results of their actions fairly quickly. You know, so if you sow a seed and it germinates, you prick it out, plant it out, you either, you either get a flower or you get a fruit, which satisfies a number of different things in people. If something goes wrong, or there's not enough care invested at any stage of that, then you won't get an end result." (organiser, project for people with mental ill health)

Although seedlings and plants require care to thrive, if that was denied them or inappropriate action taken, then their subsequent demise could also be used to demonstrate that mistakes could be made and these could be used as learning experiences. For example, some clients with mental health problems were said to be "terrified" of making mistakes and project staff could show that such errors and omissions were part of normal human behaviour and not subject to fearful consequences or sanctions. Indeed, the concept of 'surviving mistakes' was a guiding principle of one of the projects visited.

Observations about nature frequently led to expressions of deeper emotional views or attachments to the natural environment. Clients reported a 'connectedness' with nature, an awareness of its changing form throughout the year – the passage of the seasons and the changing weather:

> "I really like being in touch with the earth and the seasons and the weather, and being part of the growth cycle, and, you know, coming in in the morning and wondering if your seeds have germinated yet, and whether one of your plants is flowering yet. There were lots of things to see each day and people would take delight if they'd found something that had suddenly come into flower and looked really beautiful." (Maureen, project client with mental ill health)

> "You're dealing with nature, and these days so many of our jobs have got nothing to do with nature. It's all so artificial, like working with computers and, erm, or working with machinery and admin work, and all that sort of thing. It's good to get back to nature, and perhaps that's a bit of a corny phrase, but I think it is." (Kevin, project client with multiple disabilities)

Such an emotional bond could be taken to have a spiritual meaning. However, none of the clients made any overt spiritual or religious references or any references to any supernatural or metaphysical belief system. When one client was asked directly whether gardening and being outdoors had a spiritual significance, she replied that it did not, but that she did feel a spiritual bond with nature while out walking in the hills and mountains. Spiritual meanings and experiences of gardening have been described in the literature. These have tended to be associated with older people (see, for example, Heliker at al, 2000), and those suffering major or terminal illness (see Unruh et al, 2000; Unruh, 2004). Few older people participated in the research described here and there were no clients with major physical illness. It is also possible that there is a difference in the understanding of what constitutes 'spiritual' between researchers who carry out work into the perceived meaning of nature, and also among those who participate in garden projects. McSherry and Cash (2004) have recently reviewed the literature on the meaning of spirituality, and have examined the way in which spirituality is addressed in the context of nursing. They have produced a taxonomy of definitions ranging from the 'old traditional form' of spirituality, which is based on religious and theist beliefs, to a 'new post-modern form', which is much more inclusive and "contains an infinite number of descriptors that may be phenomenological and existentially determined such as meaning and purpose in life, creativity, and relationships" (McSherry and Cash, 2004, p 157). Such definitions of spirituality are based on individual beliefs and personal viewpoints and include concepts such as connectedness with nature, the environment and other people. Indeed, Unruh (2004) included 'connectedness to nature' and 'connectedness to others' as part of her spiritual theme in addition to the obvious concept of 'connectedness to a higher being, God'.

Other authors have also argued that finding meaning and purpose within activities, including occupational therapy, provides a spiritual dimension to people's lives (see Egan and Delaat, 1994; Howard and Howard, 1997). The feeling of being a part of nature and having a purpose within it, and of carrying out meaningful activities in the garden project can, therefore, be taken to be a spiritual dimension within the context of the modern definition of spirituality. One difficulty that remains, however, is that the modern concept of spirituality is becoming so broad, as McSherry and Cash point out, that it is in danger of losing its meaning and many different perceptions, concepts and emotions could be spuriously assigned to a spiritual meaning. Yet this may not be a problem in this case, since the modern concept of spirituality is largely individualistic and involvement in nature and a garden project may satisfy a personal emotional need that is seen as spiritual by some.

Nature and spirituality have frequently been linked together in research on perceptions of wilderness and it is interesting that in this research one of the few overt references to spirituality occurs in the context of wilderness:

"Yeah, it's nature, being outside. But what we try and do [...]. Well, I think one thing that has brought a spirituality for folks is that we're starting to do John Muir Awards here, erm, which is just looking at wilderness, looking at nature and what it does to you, and there's a lot of spirituality within that, doing story telling, visualisation, looking in a different way.

"I think spirituality is quite tied into your senses, as well. It's a mixture of mind and senses, so if you can pull those two together, then people start to think a lot more about their spirituality, how their mind is." (volunteer, project for people with mental ill health)

The aim of the John Muir Award scheme is to encourage people to discover and conserve 'wild places' in the UK. However, only one project in the research programme was involved in the scheme and although others were actively engaged in conservation work they were not specifically seeking out wilderness areas.

A theme closely associated with the emotional bond to nature was the bond to the garden or project site itself. This was often indistinguishable from the perceived connectedness to nature, as the garden site frequently symbolised nature for both clients and staff who spoke about the beauty or tranquillity of the space. The garden also had a personal meaning to clients, which could be either independent of its natural setting or connected to it, as the following three brief quotes illustrate:

"It feels like your own private space." (Tom, project client with learning difficulties)

"I find it very healing place, for myself as well. And I do think there's a lot of healing. I find it very special place, you know, we're in nature, beautiful setting, beautiful people that run it, a lot of love around the place, and I just find that everyone is healing in their own way." (Brian, project client with history of substance misuse)

"So, now, it has become part of me. So, now, it has become part of me. I don't want to leave actually. There is only the thing that, [...] they don't let stay [...], I can't stay here at night time, [laughter] overnight. Believe me. [laughter] Yes." (Tariq, project client, refugee and victim of torture)

The needs of garden maintenance and of horticulture in general ensured that clients, staff and volunteers frequently engaged in the same tasks and wore similar outdoor work clothes. Only one project had a special uniform for its staff and only a few projects required their managers to be involved only in administrative tasks and not to take on any garden activities. This was considered by some members of staff to be a 'democratising' effect, that is, in the garden all were equal and although the role of staff was to assist clients, members of staff were keen to report that they learned from clients. Overt distinctions between 'therapist' and 'client' were deliberately minimised in many cases:

> "You know, that this is normal activities that normal people do. Yeah, and the more normal the environment you're in, I mean, you know, the way we work here is very low key. It's not like therapists and clients, we muck in, you know what I mean? Although people will come to you, they know who you are if they need you, to come to you, and you'll check people out, but then pretty much you muck in, you know...." (Lisa, volunteer, project for people with mental ill health)

The outdoor environment was considered to be conducive to counselling (both formal and informal). This could be carried on while client and therapist worked together on a common task. Such an arrangement facilitated conversation because when the client was unable or unwilling to discuss his or her problems or needs it was easy to fall back on 'gardening talk'.

Conclusion

Clients expressed a preference to be outside; this appeared to be not only an escape from the 'inside' and its associated restrictions but a desire to be in the natural environment. Indeed, the natural, green environment was preferred to the outdoor city environment with its concomitant noise and traffic. The garden environment was perceived as peaceful and often imbued with a special personal meaning such as a sense of ownership, that is, "your own private space" or a place of healing. Clients and staff frequently felt a deep emotional attachment to nature and to the garden space as the embodiment of nature. Such an attachment could be viewed as a spiritual bond within the context of the modern understanding of spirituality. These findings suggest that clients' experience of 'being outside' is multifaceted.

The natural environment appears to serve as a 'restorative environment' within the framework of attention restoration theory as proposed by Kaplan and Kaplan (1989; see also Kaplan, 1995). It has the dimensions of 'being away', that is, in a different world or environment which has 'coherence' and 'extent'. The world makes sense, it is part of a greater entity which can be imagined or mapped. It provides 'fascination', it requires little effort to observe and captures attention. Clients and staff speak of their joy and pleasure at seeing plants grow and they take the trouble and effort to facilitate that growth (some of the clients used the terms 'fascinating' and 'amazing' to describe their emotions at seeing plants and nature). It has 'compatibility', that is, the project participants appear to enjoy the environment and their experiences within it. They have chosen to be within that environment, for although many clients are referred to the project by health and social care practitioners, they are under no duress to stay. Thus the outdoor, natural environment provides the emotional or psychological backdrop for the many activities and processes of STH.

The social dimension of gardening projects

Understanding the social benefits to vulnerable clients of participation in STH projects was a key objective of this study. It was clear that outcomes here would be difficult to gauge through simple observation and without the inclusion of specific questions in both the structured questionnaire and during interviews with clients. Where verbal responses would be less easily collated, for example, where clients have serious cognitive and/or communication impairments, other, participatory methods were used (see page 100).

The use of specific questions such as, 'Has the project helped you to make new friends?' and others relating to the nature and extent of significant friendships, as well as the degree of social activity with other clients outside the project, meant that it was possible to gauge the nature of the role projects played in the lives of all representative vulnerable groups in creating and developing social networks and confederacy among clients.

We know that vulnerable adults are often socially excluded from local communities either because of their circumstances, the nature of their vulnerability, or their available support systems, and so on. Thus, people with serious mental health problems or learning difficulties often have limited opportunities to make new friends outside their residential setting, or have restricted opportunities to interact fully in community life. The same is often also true of other groups such as older people or those with chronic illness. Often the only social contact these latter groups have is in health or medical settings (as outpatients at hospitals or during visits to local surgeries, for example). Furthermore, vulnerable groups such as these often only interact with others in the same situation or age group (those with dementia, Alzheimer's and other degenerative conditions, for example, often only mix with others who have similar conditions).

The formation of new and significant friendships

Key areas for investigation in the study were to ascertain whether clients used STH projects to make new friends or friendships that were particularly significant to them. As we can see from Table 4.3, most clients make a few or more friends at projects and the majority make friendships that have significance for them (see Table 4.4). Across the range of represented groups, most had benefited from project attendance by making new friends. However, comparing two particularly vulnerable groups, those clients with mental health problems were less likely to form significant friendships (40% said they had made 'none' or 'very few') than those with learning difficulties (16.6%). We know that people with mental health problems are more likely to live independently in local communities and that they often experience stigma and discrimination in these contexts (see Aldridge and Becker, 2003). This may have inevitable impacts on their capacity to trust others and socialise readily.

Table 4.3: Has the project helped you to make new friends?

Number of new friends	Frequency of responses	%
None	2	1.7
Very few	3	2.5
A few	38	31.9
Quite a lot	48	40.3
A lot	28	23.5
Total	**119**	**100.0**

Table 4.4: Has the project helped you to make special friends?

Number of special friends	Frequency of responses	%
None	16	16.7
Very few	19	14.0
A few	60	52.6
Quite a lot	12	10.5
A lot	7	6.1
Total	**114**	**100.0**

However, overall, STH projects do offer clients opportunities to develop new social contacts and to form friendships that have meaning for them. In many cases such opportunities are provided in an environment different from those that clients may be used to in their everyday lives, for example in day care facilities or residential care settings. In this respect, gardening projects also offer clients the chance to mix with new acquaintances with whom they share common interests and who may or may not have the same or similar health problems or vulnerabilities. Equally, clients may also share the desire for labour or activity that is different from the type of work they might usually undertake, as well as the need to be outside or away from their regular environment (see page 43). It seems that clients often welcome this change in their environment and the opportunity to meet friends while engaged in tasks that are both diverse and engaging.

It is clear that friendships that are formed through attendance at STH projects, and the type and range of activities clients participate in together, become important or significant in respect of the lives of vulnerable clients and they often come to rely on the regular contact with these new friends:

> "It's the fact that everybody is coming together and working together, and getting out and having a chit chat, and that....
>
> "So they've got the, erm, the friendship, companionship, erm, and also the interest. They don't feel that they're just sitting there doing nothing, just getting bored. They've actually got something to work towards." (Pete, project organiser, project for people with mental ill health)

Extending social networks

A further aim of our investigation was to understand the extent to which clients socialised with each other outside the project, or used the social skills gained at projects (including increased self-esteem and confidence) in wider contexts. Evidence of clients developing and increasing their social networks outside projects would be a further indicator of the effectiveness of STH in promoting social inclusion for vulnerable groups in diverse social contexts. However, it became clear that clients often used the projects as their main or only opportunity for socialising and the friendships made at projects were rarely sustained beyond clients' attendance at projects.

In respect of some client groups, this may be indicative of the socially restrictive or confined nature of clients' lives more generally – many of the clients who participated in the study did not live independently. A further influence here may be the fact that people with learning difficulties and serious mental health problems in particular tend to be isolated or marginalised in local communities, or protected in formal care settings. As one project organiser explained, many clients are protected or "nurtured in ways that mean if they've always had everything done for them and given to them, they think that's their right". One of the ways in which projects can help to promote social inclusion is to try and challenge and overcome clients' tendencies to be dependent on others, particularly formal health and social care practitioners.

However, in attempting to promote and foster new and significant friendships among clients, it is important that projects do not simply exchange one form of dependency or reliance for another. That is, project staff should try to ensure that the friendships that are formed at projects do not reflect the insular or over-reliant nature of friendship groups that may already prevail in clients' lives outside projects (for example, in institutional settings). Thus, where appropriate, projects should offer clients opportunities to be flexible and adaptable in the nature of the friendships they make in order for clients to develop their social skills in wider contexts (that is, outside the project). One client told us that attending his local gardening project had offered him the chance to become less insular and introverted and to mix with other people, but that he did not have any other friends and that the ones he had made at the project "are the only people I mix with". Another client said:

> **"The people who come here, we've all had the same sort of experience and the people outside that don't understand ... when we're in here all together we have a good laugh and that and that's something you can't do outside." (Donald, project client with mental ill health)**

In order to successfully promote social inclusion for vulnerable clients project staff should try to ensure that what clients are learning socially – the skills they are developing to mix with and work alongside others through gardening and related activities – they can also use outside the confines of the project. Often, the process of gardening itself can help promote social interaction and inclusion. As one client said, "The project has given me the confidence to converse with other people. When [neighbours] say come and look at my garden I can talk to them about it".

Our evidence here points to a number of other ways in which STH projects help to promote social interaction and inclusion more broadly:

- the key role of project organisers and staff;
- the planning and allocation of tasks and activities;
- the promotion of team and small group work;
- the representation and integration of clients in local communities.

The role of project organisers and staff

In many respects, project organisers and other staff play a pivotal role in accommodating and promoting the individual and social needs of clients with broader project (and client) objectives. Clients themselves often form significant associations with project organisers or staff. In this respect, the relationship may be more one-sided (although not unreciprocated) on the part of the client. Thus, while a particular project organiser, for example, may become important to a client as a 'friend', the project organiser themselves must in a sense 'befriend' all of his or her clients. This is particularly the case where clients have learning difficulties, as they often need the reassurance of a familiar and dependable person in their lives (and especially so once outside their familiar environment). It is not unusual for this person to be the organiser of the gardening project. We discuss in more detail the findings relating to people with learning difficulties and the importance of socialising and friendships to them, as evidenced in the photographic participation data (see page 100).

Project staff not only help to nurture and maintain social skills and friendships among clients, but also intervene and mediate where necessary in friendships and friendship groups in order to maintain the equilibrium of the whole. This sometimes means project organisers must intervene at times in order to ensure groups are not disrupted or fractured by the behaviour of one individual.

At times, promoting the importance of the 'team' among clients becomes necessary in order to maintain harmony and also, as the following example illustrates, in order to support individuals whose behaviour could be problematic or disruptive to the whole. Here, project organiser John describes how he intervened when Ken, a client with severe learning difficulties, became disruptive within the group *and at home* as a result of his attendance at the project. In this respect the needs of the team in terms of promoting social integration and inclusion were as important as the needs of an individual client (Ken):

> "You know we did contain [Ken] quite well and managed his problems here, but we were sort of building him up a bit too much and giving him too much confidence. He was going back home and he was saying to his mum, basically, 'Oh you can't talk to me like that. I'm a big strong man. I do lots of work at [the project]. And, you know: you can go and 'f' off'. And in this particular case, what we have to do now is make him much more part of the group rather than sort of singling him out almost as being anybody special. He still comes a couple of days a week. If he thinks he's anybody special then it goes to his head a little bit and then he's, you know, he's this big, sort of superhero figure and he can do what he wants, you know." (John, project organiser, project for people with learning difficulties)

The planning and allocation of tasks and activities

In order to ensure that clients are developing social and other skills at projects, most project staff also evaluate and monitor client progress and needs. In the companion guide to this report we discuss assessment and evaluation processes in more detail (Sempik et al, 2005). In order to ensure clients gain the most benefit from attending projects, project staff must understand the individual needs of clients as well as consider broader project objectives. This means that project staff should try to accommodate the individual needs of clients in terms of the types of activities they are both able and want to undertake as well as their abilities and willingness to mix with and work well alongside others. Project staff should also consider the extent and type of gardening and related activities required on any given day, in order to ensure project sustainability. However, most project organisers told us that clients' needs were prioritised when planning and allocating activities. Furthermore, client progress was often considered to be a gradual process that took time and effort on the part of project staff as well as the clients themselves.

In many cases, and particularly in respect of understanding the social skills of individual clients, project staff considered the shift from isolated or socially excluded individual to fully integrated member of the project with the ability (and self-confidence) to use their developing social skills outside the confines of projects, to be a gradual process and one that required time and careful planning and intervention. As one project organiser explained,

> "*To begin with*, it's getting people out, getting people out of the home, mixing with other people, being in an environment that feels quite safe, quite secure. They know there's always workers, and all, around. Erm, they're amongst other people who've experienced mental ill health. (John, project organiser, project for people with mental ill health; our emphasis)

> "[The clients] have got to help one another so that stops them being so insular because some can be. It teaches a lot of social skills, and working in a team is quite a hard thing to do, actually, and each team member seems to know what their role is and then really gel together. Now, they didn't when they first came." (Karen, project manager, project for people with learning difficulties)

In some cases, the types of activities in which clients wish to participate relate directly to their education, training or employment needs and we talk about these issues in more detail in the practice guide (see Sempik et al, 2005).

The promotion of team and small group work

In the majority of cases, gardening projects offer clients opportunities to work in a team, on their own, or with small groups of people. Many projects also give clients the opportunity to work out of doors doing gardening, construction or repair work, for example, work in the greenhouse or polytunnel, contract work (where clients go out as a group to do gardening work for local businesses or private home owners) and sometimes indoor craft work. At one such project for people with learning difficulties small groups formed quite naturally in which clients mostly undertook one type of activity or another. For example, a group of male clients worked regularly on contracts outside the project base, undertaking gardening jobs for local businesses and agencies. Another group formed, made up of mostly women who wanted to work indoors in the craft cabin (pressing flowers and leaves from the project garden to use in making greetings cards, which were later sold to the public).

In some cases, individual clients who do not form obvious firm friendships – often because of the nature of their disability or health problem – become integrated into the group through the motivation of others within it. In their work with patients with severe and enduring mental illness, Perrins-Margalis et al (2000) also noted the importance of group motivation: "Participants described the group as a team. The group provided reinforcement for those participants who were less motivated to do the activity" (p 22). This is illustrated in our research by the following case study:

Case history: Geoff

Geoff is 64 and has schizophrenia. He has been attending the gardening project (which specialises in horticultural training) for only four months. One of the project organisers described Geoff as uncommunicative and inactive when he first attended the project, but over the few months he had been attending had become more sociable with project staff and other clients. Geoff's physical activity hadn't increased to any great extent, but his sociability, integration in the group and willingness to learn had been noticeable. Sean, the project organiser and a community mental health worker, has known Geoff for many years and has observed the changes in him:

"At first there was quite a lot of pressure for Geoff to move into residential care. But certainly in the last two or three years he's had quite a steady improvement [while he's been here]. He gets very involved at his own pace every week as there are particular jobs that he likes more than others, erm, but it's through talking to him recently, he's very happy to do the jobs that he's not so keen on, as well."

"Because he sees it as education. He sees it as learning new skills. Somebody towards the back end of last growing season saw him taking lots of food home. Normally all his food is prepared by carers. He hasn't had much of a say in what he eats. He can go home, there's food prepared in the fridge all ready to go in the microwave. So he started taking food home. And initially he was demanding that people cook it for him. As a consequence of being here, he wanted a men's cookery group, cooking produce that he'd grown. So he's really enjoyed eating food that he's produced himself."

"He really shone in the classroom sessions too, and he really, really shone. It's very difficult to understand what he's saying a lot of the time, because he's really quite slurred. He puts himself down a lot, but we just could not shut him up. In the question and answer sessions in the classroom, he was fabulous. Erm, and got lots and lots of praise by it, and lots of, erm, positive response from everybody else on the course." (Sean, project organiser, project for people with mental ill health)

The *desire* to cooperate is often an important element of team work. Frequently in the modern workplace, because of the pressures of work, voluntary cooperation between work colleagues is absent or limited to well-defined groups with specific allegiances. Furthermore, as we have said, vulnerable clients and service users who are institutionalised often lack the opportunity to work closely alongside others in a team with a common goal. The diverse range of activities on offer at projects, the lack of pressure to perform (see page 68) and the opportunities to work in teams or small groups may all be factors that help promote voluntary cooperation. As one project organiser said,

"I think it's probably because, you know, people aren't put under pressure and it's much easier to cooperate if someone's not badgering you all the time and, erm, harking on about quality control, I mean, just all that sort of [...]. It's about space and, you know, if you shove [...] it's a bit like, you know, trying to bring ten kids up in a, erm, a two-bedroomed house. You know, it would be chaos and, you know, you move into a ten-bedroomed house and life's much easier, and it's a bit the same. People have room here to grow and recover whereas in their normal environments they haven't. Erm, and I think that's quite special, really." (Phil, project organiser, project for people with mental ill health)

Issues relating to teamwork are also discussed on page 95 in the context of self-esteem and self-confidence.

The representation and integration of clients in local communities

> **"Part of the value of what we do, it's like social inclusion and integration within the community, and that's an important part of what we do. And being visible out on contracts, that's showing the public that people with disabilities can make a difference and they can have a contribution within the community. And so we're, like educating the public as well." (Keith, project organiser, project for people with learning difficulties)**

One of the key roles gardening projects play in promoting social inclusion is in integrating vulnerable adults – those who are mostly socially *excluded* – in local communities, and helping to overcome the prejudice about, or stereotyping of, for example, people with learning difficulties or serious mental health problems. Promoting social inclusion through representation and integration may not be an a priori, or purposive strategy of all gardening projects but may occur, for example, as a result of geography (the physical locality of projects) and/or the nature of the client base.

Projects whose clients are particularly vulnerable – those with learning difficulties or mental health problems, for example – often benefit from being situated close to private residences or in urban areas where local people can see the work that clients do on a daily basis and the contributions they make to the wider community. Furthermore, local residents can become more involved in the work of projects in this respect. Where projects are based on allotment sites, clients often work alongside other local plot holders who share a common interest in horticulture.

One of the projects included in the in-depth study of STH projects had been established 14 months earlier in a local community directly on the edge of a river and water treatment site, but also on the edge of a private housing estate. The project organiser said that initially local people objected to the establishment of the gardening project (whose clients were people with learning difficulties), and, once the project was set up, had then insisted on the removal of one of the greenhouses, which they said obstructed their view of the river. The project organiser also told us that local people were 'wary of the clients'. Other projects for people with learning difficulties and mental health problems also experienced similar difficulties in respect of the perceptions and misconceptions of people in local communities about vulnerable groups. As one project organiser said:

> **"You've only got to scratch the surface and that prejudice is there. But then as soon as you've, you know, made your presence known, and people realise you're not all ogres ... people very quickly sort of warm to the group and because you've got this common interest like horticulture." (Keith, project organiser, project for people with learning difficulties)**

By making clients visible in local communities, by representing their interests and promoting social integration, STH projects play an important role in helping to challenge prejudice, challenge misconceptions and in broadening the social skills of vulnerable clients. There are a number of identifiable ways in which clients benefit socially, in a broader sense, from attending STH projects. These include:

- Being involved in promotion and marketing, in particular, project plant sales and seed swaps. These allow clients opportunities to meet the public and to engage with local residents, and others, who visit the project to buy produce and exchange goods and ideas.
- Interacting with local residents who share a common interest in gardening, as one client said, "[The project is] good for social reasons as well because you know we've got gardens across the fence there. You know, they come and chat to us, they borrow plants and you know, borrow compost and we give them stuff".
- Participating in contract work for local businesses or private home owners. This is an important factor in promoting social inclusion through representation and integration as it enables clients to demonstrate their skills publicly and to interact with local people in diverse settings. As one project organiser explained, when describing the importance of contract work, "Taking clients out and in and around the local area and getting them to garden, just like everyone else does, and show what they can do in the garden, is [important for] social inclusion and integration within the community, and that's an important part of what we do".
- Working alongside others and providing support. Projects that are situated on allotment sites (for example) inevitably involve clients working alongside other private plot holders. This means, once again, that clients are visible, represented and can demonstrate their own gardening skills. In some cases, clients also help other plot holders with gardening tasks, as one project organiser explained, "I mean, what we're doing at the moment, talking about normalisation, there's a chap up here on that allotment who ... he lays on his side to garden, his back is so bad, and we're giving him half an hour of our time. So, that's just showing, like, help other people, and there's other people with different disabilities".

The social benefits for specific groups

Gender and ethnicity

> **Her themes were infatuation with natural beauty, a romantic desire to be left alone in her garden undisturbed by household duties, and frustration at having to employ gardeners instead of being allowed to work in the soil herself. (Kellaway, 1996, p x, describing gardener Elizabeth Von Arnim)**

Women have been professional gardeners for many years; names such as Elizabeth von Arnim and Gertrude Jekyll are familiar to many as pioneers of women's early involvement in gardening and horticulture. Women also commonly participate in domestic gardening activity and recent research has suggested that the garden has a significant role to play for women in respect of providing an extension of homemaking activity and as a place where gender relations are augmented. Bhatti and Church (2000) have suggested, "the gendered meanings of gardens and the garden as a place where gender power relations are played out, are highly significant in the social construction of 'home'" (Bhatti and Church, 2000, p 183).

Some research suggests that gardening and horticulture activity can be beneficial to particular groups of clients, for example, women and black and minority ethnic groups. However, some studies, as well as our own research here, indicate that these particular groups are also under-represented at STH projects (see Naidoo et al, 2001; Sempik et al, 2005).

Evidence from national surveys and from our in-depth survey of projects shows that the ratio of female to male clients attending STH projects is 30:70 (%). Women and black and minority ethnic groups are also under-represented across the range of client groups. Furthermore, the percentage of women-only projects across the UK (who are members of Thrive's network of projects) represents just 2.4%, and the number of black and minority ethnic groups is 4.3%. A number of factors may account for such low representation, although given what little research is available in this area, it is possible only to speculate and hypothesise about the reasons for under-representation here.

First, it must be remembered that the nature and location of STH projects are different from those in domestic contexts. Research tends to focus on the latter where, as Bhatti and Church have further suggested, "gender relations may be reinforced or renegotiated" (Bhatti and Church, 2000, p 183). However, STH projects are inevitably set aside from private, domestic space and tend to be at dedicated locations to which clients travel. But, irrespective of location, if the garden is also a "place and space, and is related to the act of cultivation, that is, gardening" (Bhatti and Church, 2000, p 183), then we can suppose that STH projects offer the same opportunities and outcomes for all groups, regardless of gender or race.

Second, it must be remembered that what distinguishes all groups in respect of the type of client groups who attend STH projects is the nature of their particular vulnerability. Clients are not referred to projects on the basis of their gender or race but on the basis of their illness, disability or factors that lead to their social exclusion or isolation. It could be that health and social care practitioners who make referrals to STH projects are making gender or cultural assumptions about particular client groups and their abilities or preferences, but our evidence suggests this is unlikely. The reasons underlying practitioner referral are explained in other ways, for example the nature and extent of practitioner caseloads, as one occupational therapist commented:

> "I've referred more men, but then I think, on my caseload I do have more men anyway, so that's probably the reason rather than any particular suitability ... any particular bias in terms of whether females or males would like to, erm, like to go there. Right. I think it's also perhaps, you know, perhaps, the, not just on my caseload, more men than women, but also, perhaps the more damaged clients, the more chronic clients, are also, the men, just happens to be my caseload at the moment."

Indeed, most health and social care practitioners and STH project staff we spoke to said that referral procedures were based on talking to clients and meeting their individual needs, based on their own wishes and preferences. However, only a small number of health and social care professionals were interviewed for this research and further investigation would be valuable in this area.

Third, if domestic gardening is indeed evidence of an extension of homemaking responsibility – which is traditionally and culturally associated with women – then it is precisely the nature of STH projects, and the types of gardening and horticulture activities that they offer, that may serve to discourage some women (including those from black and minority ethnic groups) from using them for therapeutic purposes. However, for others, the opportunities STH projects provide for extending social networks and interaction will be seen as one of the advantages of attending these projects. More single, divorced or separated women use STH projects than those who are married or living with a partner. This might suggest that women who do not have partners may be using STH projects more for the social opportunities they provide, and the chance to participate in activities alongside others who may be in similar situations to themselves, rather than the opportunity to enhance their homemaking skills.

However, gender may be significant here in other ways. For example, the predominance of male clients at projects may serve to discourage some women from joining STH projects, especially vulnerable women and those from black and minority ethnic groups. As one project organiser explained, "I think, as well, a female coming into mostly a male organisation is quite daunting for them, a lot to take in".

Indeed there may be a clue here as to how and why women benefit socially and culturally from the *exclusive* nature of women-only projects, or projects for women from black and minority ethnic groups, for example. Research from the US and from our own in-depth study on women who attend dedicated, women-only projects, and sessions, tells us that there are a number of benefits to be gained from STH outside the more generic positive outcomes that relate to all client groups. These are:

- solidarity and like-mindedness;
- security and safety;
- freedom from discrimination, stereotype and patriarchy.

Solidarity, security and freedom from discrimination

Some research has suggested that gender can be a significant factor in how individuals experience horticulture. Unruh et al (2000) studied female patients' experiences of gardening as a therapy following treatment for cancer. The authors concluded that these women's reflections about gardening and experiences of illness were "more characteristic of women" and that men who garden would "raise different issues" (Unruh et al, 2000, p 76). One of the ways in which women (including those from black and minority ethnic groups) benefit from attending gender and culture-specific STH projects, or sessions (some generic projects offer women-only sessions), is in the experience and expression of solidarity. The Green Gym allotment project operating in the North of England offers women from local communities the opportunity to relax, rejuvenate, work alongside nature and 'meet like-minded women'.

In the US, Powch's research on wilderness therapy (see Sempik et al, 2003) aimed to "include the voices of women of color and other marginalized groups of women" (Powch, 1994, p 13). She was looking for an additional 'ingredient' in her research that was empowering for women. She concluded that notions of unity and female solidarity were distinct outcomes for women who shared wilderness therapy. She further suggested that feminist spirituality and creativity were enhanced by women's collective experiences of the wilderness:

> **Wilderness therapy appears to be a promising vehicle for empowerment of women. Its promise is not limited to being a vehicle by which women can master skills that enhance self-esteem and a sense of control. Its promise is much greater and goes beyond the personal when it is connected with the feminist spirituality movement and reclamation of the earth as a woman's place, woman as creator and a part of the spirit of the earth. (Powch, 1994, p 25)**

This same sense of solidarity and enhancement of personal skills and self-esteem is clearly evident in the data from our in-depth investigation of projects, in particular from data collected at a project for women from black and minority ethnic communities in the North East of England. The women use the project to grow and consume their own produce, to meet socially, develop their language skills and to work alongside one another in a safe environment, as the project organiser explained:

> **"It's a supportive environment. [The women] can support each other and it builds confidence and empowers them and there are skills that they've used here and on other gardens."**

Many of the women who attend these projects have experienced discrimination and social exclusion because of their ethnicity, their gender and also because they are made more vulnerable by their illness or disability. Some of them have also experienced physical, sexual or emotional abuse and being part of a women-only group, and particularly one which is also culturally relevant to their own experiences, can help them to feel more secure in both the natural environment and in local communities, where in many cases they are fearful of harassment or abuse.

> **"[One of the aims of the project is] social cohesion because [the women] are out there and they're working in a place where lots of other groups work and it breaks down people's attitudes and a lot of stereotypes ... this is a pretty tough area and people see this sort of group working away there and you know, it just makes people think. It's challenging in a subtle way, if you like." (Angela, project organiser, project for women from black and minority ethnic communities)**

Frederickson and Anderson's (1999) purposive study of women's experiences of wilderness therapy described positive outcomes for women in terms of increased equanimity and cohesion. They also found that, for vulnerable women (for example, survivors of sexual abuse) the collective experience of the natural environment could offer physical and emotional safety as well as personal bonding. 'Escape from stereotype' was also a factor for some women, and this is also reflected in our findings.

Most of the women who attended one of the dedicated projects in our study (for women from black and minority ethnic communities) welcomed the opportunity to get together with other women away from the family home and from social and cultural expectations. Most of them also said they preferred to attend a dedicated women-only project:

> **"We can talk easily, we can, joke about everything, because in our culture we can't make any jokes in front of the males. [We can] enjoy ourselves, just talking and giving and getting ideas." (Padma, project client, women's organic gardening project)**

Even when STH projects do not offer dedicated services for particular groups (for example, women and people from black and minority ethnic communities) there are a number of strategies that can help promote equality of opportunity and representation that will mean these groups can benefit in the ways we have outlined here, as well as in other ways that promote social inclusion. For example, at the referral stage, projects can take positive steps to ensure clients are equally represented in terms of gender and cultural background (see Naidoo et al, 2001). Some projects offer dedicated women-only sessions or group work that ensures people of similar backgrounds can work alongside one another. We talk in more detail about some of these strategies in *Growing together* (Sempik et al, 2005).

Conclusion

It is clear that STH projects have an important role to play in encouraging the formation of friendships between clients and helping to develop their social skills. For particularly vulnerable adults, for example, those with learning difficulties, the friendships formed while attending STH sessions are important because they often have limited opportunities to make new friends in their daily lives. People with learning difficulties are often isolated and excluded from a society that does not always fully understand their needs or the fact that they have important contributions to make.

While all groups in the study benefited socially from attending STH projects, specific groups such as vulnerable women and people from minority ethnic communities could benefit more broadly from increased referrals to projects and from other positive strategies, for example, women-only sessions and monitoring intake in order to ensure more equal representation of under-represented groups.

Issues relating to work and employment

Many horticultural projects offer programmes of training for future employment; some also provide activities and structures that resemble formal employment. The importance of work and employment as a goal for project trainees has also been reported in the literature. Indeed, in our recent review of the literature on STH (Sempik et al, 2003) we commented on the role that work, or activities that provide a substitute for work, may have in engendering well-being for some groups of individuals. There has been a great deal of research on the psychological benefits that work provides and these are generally grouped under the heading of the 'meaning of work'. Morse and Weiss (1955) were among the first authors to report empirical evidence that work had a function beyond the provision of financial security. They noted that:

> **... for most men working does not simply function as a means of earning a livelihood. Even if there were no economic necessity for them to work, most men would work anyway. (Morse and Weiss, 1955, p 198)**

This observation was based on interviews with a total of 401 employed men from different occupations and backgrounds. Eighty per cent of those taking part in the study responded that they would continue to work even if they inherited sufficient money to live comfortably without working. Work provided a meaning and function for employed people – being part of something, having something interesting to do and also the opportunity for social contact. It also provided a framework to prevent inactivity, particularly for those in physical and manual jobs:

> **Working class occupations emphasize work with tools, operation of machines, lifting, carrying, and the individual is probably orientated to the effort rather than the end. Therefore life without working becomes life without anything to do. (Morse and Weiss, 1955, p 195)**

A study by Vecchio (1980), 25 years later, showed that the majority of people would still wish to continue working even if they had no financial need to do so, although this number had fallen to 72% of those questioned. It is likely that the attitudes to work have continued to change but that work is still important for the majority of people inasmuch as it provides benefits other than financial remuneration.

Much subsequent research has looked at the meaning of work in the context of the psychological effects of unemployment. It is clear that unemployment is associated with negative psychological effects and poor mental health including depression, anxiety, general distress and lowered self-confidence and self-esteem, although there has been disagreement concerning the mechanisms that cause or facilitate these effects. Jahoda (1979) has argued that employment and the working environment provide a latent support, that is, unintended consequences of work for employed people in the form of five key dimensions, namely:

> **employment imposes a time structure on the waking day ... employment implies regularly shared experiences and contacts with people outside the nuclear family ... employment links an individual to goals and purposes which transcend his [sic] own ... employment defines aspects of personal status and identity ... employment enforces activity. (Jahoda, 1979, p 313; for a review and critique of the literature on unemployment see Fryer and Payne, 1986)**

Loss of employment can lead to *deprivation* in meeting the individuals' needs and consequent destructive physical and psychological effects. In a similar vein, Warr (1987) proposed a model of nine environmental factors associated with mental health and well-being (these have sometimes been likened to 'vitamins' for mental health). This model could be applied both to those in employment and also to unemployed people since activities and environments not related to work could also supply these 'vitamins'. The nine factors that Warr identified were:

- opportunity for control;
- opportunity for skill use;
- externally generated goals;
- variety;
- environmental clarity;
- availability of money;
- physical security;
- opportunity for interpersonal contact;
- valued social position.

It is useful to compare these environmental factors with the key dimensions of social inclusion – *production, consumption, political engagement* and *social interaction* proposed by Burchardt et al (2002). A considerable degree of overlap appears to exist between these two sets of proposed dimensions. Is it, therefore, the latent benefits of work that contribute to social inclusion? And do horticultural projects need to be *like work* in order to promote social inclusion and other benefits?

Does project work feel like work?

Participants in the research programme were asked whether their activities at the projects *felt like work*. In other words, did they associate their involvement in the projects with their experiences of paid employment and did any benefits result from the project activities being similar to work activities?

Although all of the projects studied had a structured working day with set start and finish times and allocated break times, many of the participants did not feel that project work was similar to employment because of the lack of pressure and the enjoyable nature of the activities.

Clients were asked: How would you compare coming to the project with going to work? If you have no experience of work how do you think it may compare?

> **"There's no pressure. If you've done a job you've done it for money – a normal job, and to earn your money you have to stick at it, do everything right, make no mistakes and that's to get your money and that is like the pressure of your job, you've got to do it right." (Peter, project client, with mental ill health)**

> **"Oh, I'd sooner come here than go to work, it was either fit or factories, I won't ever go back in a factory again and I won't ever work for anybody else again, because they just use you, I've always said you're just a number and not a person, you're just a number." (Donald, project client, with mental ill health)**

A similar theme was expressed by another client with mental health problems:

> **"My time-keeping is terrible because my mornings are very bad. I have a struggle in the mornings, so I'm never on time for work. I wouldn't last a week in a proper job.**

> **"Erm, plus the sort of work. Erm, the emphasis isn't on production here, either, so it doesn't matter how much you do when you get here, whereas, at work, time is money, and it would count." (Tony, project client with mental ill health)**

One interviewee identified the lack of the burden of responsibility in making project work distinct from employment:

> **"... it doesn't have the responsibility that I would have had at work. So, for instance, I don't have to come here, for a start. If I don't [...] if I feel really bad, I don't have to come here."**

> **But you still do?**

> **"Yeah. And I can come late as well, because sometimes it may be that I don't get here until half ten whereas most people get here at half nine, so there's that element of it, yeah." (Barbara, project client, with mental ill health)**

Even when similarities between project *work* and employment were seen this was qualified:

Do you think working here is like being at work?

"[Long pause] Yes, but in the way, working in something that you want to do and you're getting a real job satisfaction out of as opposed to doing something because you've got to as a means to an end." (Cathy, volunteer/client, project for people with mental ill health, learning and other difficulties)

Project activity was therefore seen as enjoyable and in this way quite distinct from previous encounters with employment. Many clients also sought to extend their involvement with projects and some engaged in the cultivation of other gardens, including their own and those of family and friends, and some kept allotments. Some project staff also voiced their opinions that working on the projects *did not feel like work* because it was enjoyable. These staff were engaged in activities that they liked, for example art and gardening, and that they also chose as hobbies.

Project work differs from mainstream employment (in most cases) since there is no necessity to make a profit from the project's activities; this in turn removes that specific pressure from the organisers and participants. Participants reported that being engaged in project work was unlike employment because it lacked the pressures to perform productively, to be punctual, to avoid making mistakes. Indeed, the theme used by one project in counselling their clients (people with mental health problems) was *surviving mistakes* – the notion that mistakes could be made and the consequences did not matter. The following two examples illustrate this principle:

"She was somebody who was terrified of making mistakes, and if she made a mistake, you know, she would be just waiting for the sky to fall in, you know. I mean, it took a long time, but that's one of the things she says she most learned when she was here, that you could actually survive making a mistake.

"Our style of gardening is much more informal and much more forgiving, and the plants have to go, you know. If somebody ... not in this centre, actually, but a centre I worked in before, somebody with the best will in the world watered all the seedlings with water out of the boiling hot tap.

"Now, you have to say, 'Thanks for watering all the seedlings'. [laughs] You can't say, 'Oh, you've killed them all!' you know? You can point out that, 'Maybe next time you could use *that* tap', but he did what he thought was helping, you know, so you have to be prepared for that." (Sue, project organiser, project for people with mental ill health)

It is unlikely that many employers who have to return an economic profit could adopt such an attitude.

Any pressures were self-imposed. Some participants felt that by working hard they themselves would benefit and consequently set themselves personal goals, for example to finish a specific piece of work by the end of the day:

> **"I've always set myself deadlines and goals, and maybe pressurised myself, but I actually thrive under pressure. [laughs] That's what, in a way, drives me, having a deadline. I always try to [...]. I always set a deadline, even with work here: I want this finished today, or I'll do this today, and maybe if I finish that bit then I'll do something else, so I'll do a bit more. I've always done that, though, with myself, rather than just start a job with no set time for finishing, because that way you can sort of drag your heels a bit." (Tony, project client, with mental ill health)**

For the clients described above, project work *does not feel like work*. However, for some of the projects studied, productivity was important; these were the social firms and cooperatives. In some cases (social firms) the existence of the company was dependent on the ability to produce profit – as with any commercial venture. While in others (cooperatives) the project model deliberately sought to mimic employment as part of the training programme and involvement in the commercial market place underlined this. For example, one cooperative sold compost produced from garden waste and also mushrooms grown in a specially constructed polytunnel. All members of the cooperative showed an interest in the workings of the business – the cooperative had regular meetings with a formal structure and agenda. Members were involved in running the business and saw it as *their* business and took pride in it. However, there was no pressure on the business to generate an income that provided a realistic wage for members of the cooperative. Business and administration skills could be learned and practised in an unpressured environment. This lack of pressure may well have promoted the enjoyment of the project.

Work, structure and status

Employment provides a structure in the lives of those who go to work, and as mentioned above, loss of employment can lead to harmful consequences through the loss of that structure. Similarly, project activities provide a structure to the participants' lives. Most attend the projects on a regular basis – 77% of those taking part in the study reported that they attended on two or more days, with 50% attending on three days or more. Although short, typically from 9.30 or 10 in the morning until 3 or 4 in the afternoon, the working day is organised around start and finish times, lunch and tea breaks, outstanding tasks and so on. Ninety per cent of respondents in the study reported taking part in a session that lasted for four hours or longer and 53% worked for six hours or more (mean length of a project session = 5.5 hours, *n* = 125 respondents). The provision of such a structured day is the intended aim of some of the projects:

> "The aim, as we see it, is to, and our standard line is, to enable people to get back control of their lives because often people's lives have gone very out of control if they've become unwell. So, [...] and we would do that through quite simple things. It's not complicated. It's simple things like time-keeping, attendance, diet, sleep patterns. Getting control over those things helps people to then move on and do what they want to do with their lives. But if those things are out of control it's impossible for people to do anything that they want to do....

> "We start at nine o'clock, we work till lunch at half twelve, we go back to work at a quarter past one, and we ask people to do at least three days a week, so already that's quite a structure that they've committed to." (Sue, project organiser, project for people with mental ill health)

Structure may also arise from the collective efforts of the trainees. The organiser of one project did not impose a structure on the working day but considered that it arose spontaneously from the wishes and needs of the trainees:

> "Erm, tea times, erm, lunch times, and things, are not [...], there's no set time and it is quite interesting, though, that, erm, the time seems to be [...]. Everyone, you know, can [...] happens to do [...], have lunch at the same time and that's just through choice. You know, I've never said that lunch must be at twelve thirty, yet most people just do that, and there's no set time to do that, at all....

> "... We don't try and impose a structure, yet it, [...] actually, one seems to develop, an informal one develops, you know, but we'd never tell anybody they can't, you know, they can't stop now. We may encourage if we've got a big job – you know, 'Oh, let's get this finished', but, you know [...] – and then we'll have an easy afternoon, and we might have a two-hour lunch break or something, erm, but, overall, things, you know, things do get done." (Phil, organiser, project for people with mental ill health)

However, the transport requirements and arrangements of the trainees ensured regular, if not necessarily punctual, start and finish times.

Projects also provide an identity and status for the participants. Project trainees are happy to refer to themselves as 'gardeners'. Before attending their project many felt uncomfortable in 'admitting' that they were unemployed; once they became part of the project they felt pride in being able to say that they were 'gardeners':

"... it gave me an identity, a new identity, because now I could think of myself as a gardener. Otherwise I was just a patient, somebody who suffers from a mental illness. And through coming to the garden, I was a gardener, and if people asked me what I did, there wasn't the usual awkward silence while I tried to think how to put it, but I could say that I was a gardener and talk about what I'd been doing that day. And that made a fairly immediate difference.)

"... and it gave me the status of 'working', as far as other people were concerned. I didn't have to explain if I didn't want to, I didn't have to say I was on benefits and not working. I could say, well, I was working as a gardener, and didn't have to go into details, so it had the, sort of, benefits of being a bit like work in that it was your workplace that you come to." (Jane, former client and currently employee, project for people with mental ill health; see below for case history)

Case history: Jane

Jane had been a senior administrator in the NHS before becoming ill with severe depression and anxiety and was still very ill in 1996 despite medication and hospitalisation. A community psychiatric nurse suggested that she visit the project – "I know just the place for you". She immediately found a resonance with the project and its staff:

"I came here with, erm, just from very little hope. I'd, sort of, lost everything and I'd been in hospital for a long time and I didn't really see a future. But I was recommended to come here by a nurse who thought it was just the place for me, and I was lucky that, I think she must have visited the garden and knew about it. So I came on a visit and something about the place immediately engaged me. I think it was the, it was so far removed from hospital-type of services or medical-type of services and I felt that I was, on my first day here I immediately felt that I was, I was, sort of, seen as an individual and not just as a patient."

"One of the, sort of, first things, I guess, was that it gave me a structure to my day, and a routine, and I was glad to be able to come in for the day, everyday, five days a week because I find one of my big problems was that time was just so difficult to get through when I was feeling really bad."

In addition to routine, the project provided the opportunity to meet people, work together and engage in jokes and laughter. It enabled Jane to gain an identity and status. She felt that she was no longer 'just a patient' but was now a 'gardener' and had something to talk about with her friends:

> "... I could think of myself as a gardener. Otherwise I was just a patient, somebody who suffers from a mental illness. And through coming to the garden, I was a gardener, and if people asked me what I did, there wasn't the usual awkward silence while I tried to think how to put it, but I could say that I was a gardener and talk about what I'd been doing that day."

Although she says that she felt better as soon as she started the project, her improvement was a slow process. The first two years were characterised by peaks and troughs in her condition and by hospital admissions. The project staff provided intensive support including one-to-one working at the project and covered out of working hours and at weekends. They also worked closely with her mental health team.

After approximately four years at the project her condition and confidence had improved sufficiently for her to engage in voluntary work for the parent organisation – a mental health charity – and when the organisation advertised for an administrator she applied for the post and was selected. She had not worked for nine years previously and had been attending the project for around six-and-a-half years. She believes that learning new skills at the project gave her the confidence and ability to apply for the job and to carry it out successfully:

> "And I think if it hadn't been for the gardening, which had all this time been preparing me, building up my confidence, teaching me new skills, erm, being a, sort of, safe place for me to come while I was building things up for myself, erm, I don't think I would ever have been in a position where I could take on a job like this. And it's quite a challenging job. It's quite hard but I'm enjoying it."

A year later Jane is still employed full time at the project. She says that she needs the support of her colleagues and the project to work and likes to spend a couple of hours each day in the garden before starting her own job, which can be very stressful.

She describes her psychiatrist as a "medical man" who firmly believes in the power of medication. However, he does realise that the garden has a special meaning for Jane. She thinks that he may be sceptical of the benefits that she believes that the project has provided and may attribute any improvement in her condition to her medication. He has not visited the garden; although some psychiatrists and social workers visit their patients at the project, he has not done so.

For Jane the garden has been "the most important place to me in my whole life" and she lists the following dimensions of the project as having a particular contribution to her improvement: working with other people, the support of colleagues and staff, nature – the natural environment – and "having something to look after". The natural environment is especially important:

> "I really like being in touch with the earth and the seasons and the weather, and being part of the growth cycle, and, you know, coming in in the morning and wondering if your seeds have germinated yet, and whether one of your plants is flowering yet."

Jane promotes the project as a user for whom it has been beneficial. She is concerned that the patients and potential clients that she talks to may not realise the seriousness of her illness when she first started at the project, as she appears confident and well.

Project managers were also keen to emphasise the work aspects of projects rather than their therapeutic value to the clients, who were encouraged to regard coming to a project as 'going to work':

> "Everybody that comes here calls this their 'work', and I quite like to encourage that idea, that it's work and that they're capable of doing work, and, rather than [...]. I would hate to think that somebody was saying, 'Oh, I'm going to my therapy', because it's like an extension of their illness, if you like, as opposed to being a way forward from their illness. I mean, some people do [thirty] years in hospitals and [...] I mean, I'm not denying that it isn't therapeutic, it probably is, but people's perception of what they're doing when they come here is that it's their work. (Carol, project organiser, project for people with mental ill health)

A topic associated with work and status is the issue of the use of tools and machines. Projects provided clients with the opportunity to receive training in a wide variety of garden tools and machinery ranging from mowers and strimmers to chainsaws, shredders and other power tools. Once trained, they were able to use the equipment in most cases with little or no supervision and the use of such tools was an important aspect of their enjoyment of the project and sense of satisfaction. The following quote from a man with mental health problems demonstrates his enjoyment of using a lawn mower and his desire to be able to use a strimmer:

"The good thing is that I get to use a lawn mower, too.

"I'm normally cutting grass, do cutting grass, weeding, watering the plants, which I enjoy doing, watering the plants, cutting grass and weeding, and doing the mowing machine, which I like to have a shot with, and one time I used the strimmer.

"Oh, some of the staff, like ... and ... just teach me how to use a lawn mower, just how to walk up and down the grass with a lawn mower. I know how to use a lawn mower, I know how to use it all right. One machine which I never used in the past, in the two years since I've been here, is a strimmer." (Gary, project client, with mental ill health)

In addition to garden machinery some projects provided access to other equipment such as a blacksmith's forge, pole lathes and wood-turning tools. Training and the use of such tools and machinery identify the user as a 'trained or competent person' and hence confer status. Interestingly, when clients with learning difficulties were given disposable cameras so that they could photograph aspects of their project, one young man photographed a strimmer and chose that particular photograph as one of his favourites (see page 101).

Getting paid

One very important aspect of employment is remuneration – getting paid for the work carried out. While most people in paid employment take pay for granted, only some of those participating in horticultural projects received any financial reward or recompense for their efforts. There were a number of different ways in which this was paid – as travelling (and other) expenses, attendance allowance or as a share of profit in a cooperative commercial venture. In some cases the amount paid was very small, for example, 80 pence per day attendance allowance in one project. This was seen as derisory by one project worker:

"And I think partly because of [...] cares, financial difficulties at the moment, they're talking about just giving people a flat attendance allowance....

"... which will be eighty pence a day, which, really, I suppose you could say, would help towards bus fares or towards other expenses but, really, I mean, it's an insult to anybody that is working. I mean, some people, you can say, it does work as a motivator because, thinking of it, some people don't understand about money, they get a wage packet, it's something that jingles [...] and, you know, they can use that to get some magazines or sweets or whatever, but for the people that do understand about money and know the value of money and, you know, we're all

trying to develop that sort of awareness in people, it's an insult, really." (Keith, project organiser, project for people with mental ill health)

In other projects where the amount was greater, for example £15 to £20 per week in one project, and approximately £350 per year dividend in one cooperative venture, the money was seen as important. It provided a small degree of independence – those receiving the allowance could choose what they bought with the money: cigarettes, tobacco, newspapers, magazines and so on. Often those in receipt of larger amounts (profit shares) spent most or all of the money in one go on needed or desired items, for example, clothes or a computer. The act of receiving pay was regarded with significance and importance – in one project the allowances were distributed every Friday in brown 'pay packet style' envelopes and payday was eagerly awaited. Clients referred to the project as *their work*. In some cases this had caused problems. One client who was in receipt of benefit had spoken about 'going to work' and the project manager had to explain to the Benefits Agency that the client was not being paid a wage but only a small sum to cover expenses. Currently it is permissible to receive a small income up to the 'earnings disregard' limit without affecting income-related benefits (Income Support, Housing Benefit or Council Tax Benefit); however, the actual amount can vary according to individual circumstances. It is interesting that in comparison to their benefits, the *pay* was small but appeared to be of much greater significance. There was discussion about *pay* at tea breaks but not about benefit. Pay was seen as *earned* and *deserved* income that contributed to the status of the client as 'worker'.

Some clients who did not receive pay desired to be in paid employment but recognised that such work also brought pressure. This created a conflict between wanting paid employment and its associated pressures, and wanting the low-pressured environment of the project. Again, the receipt of pay was considered to be a measure of 'self-worth' and therefore a factor in the client's self-esteem:

> **"There's something about being paid, I think, being in paid work that [...] which is very hard to imitate unless you're actually paid, and [...] you know, but at the same time you have other pressures on you, as well, so it's hard to get the combination right and being paid for it, as well, without having the pressure, is very hard.**
>
> **"Yeah. But, I mean, [the project] takes together a lot of the stuff that's been [...] you know, but I still have times when I think I'm affected by not working full time in paid work only.**
>
> **"There's something about receiving the money in your hand that's, kind of, a statement of self-worth somehow." (Ken, project client, with mental ill health)**

In projects where pay was not given there were occasional (but not frequent) incidents where clients refused to carry out a task because they were not being paid. They felt there was no reason for them to do a 'job' that they disliked. Presumably had they been paid they would have simply got on with the task.

Finding paid employment

Although the stated aim of some of the projects was to enable the participants to find employment, only 30 clients reported that they were actually using the project as a means of finding paid work. Also, the reported numbers leaving projects for paid work were low, although most projects did not keep accurate records of employment rates. One project did, however, report an annual rate of 50%. The manager suggested that clients with mental health problems drifted in and out of work as their health changed; however, no records of this were kept. Three other projects reported that approximately 25%, 20% and 16% of their clients found employment. The remaining 20 projects made an estimate of 10% or fewer and 10 of these suggested that the figure was 5% or less. Some of these considered the numbers to be 'very low' or 'very rare'. Of 11 projects that were mainly for people with learning difficulties, eight reported employment rates of less than 5%. Even the efforts of a project backed by a major organisation with significant resources and links to potential employers produced a fairly modest return, with only around 10% of its clients finding paid employment. The low estimated rates of employment were matched by a low observed rate of employment. In the follow-up interviews with project managers, 9 to 12 months after the initial visit, it was found that of 137 clients in the study only one was in full-time employment outside the project, three had part-time jobs and five were employed by projects. Two of those who had found part-time employment, and three who were employed by projects, had previously stated that they were using project attendance as a means to employment (out of a total of 30 clients who had given that response in the questionnaire).

It has been reported that finding employment by those with enduring mental health problems or learning difficulties is not easy. In recent times this may have become yet more difficult. Perkins and Rinaldi (2002) recently showed that in the London Borough of Wandsworth the number of people with mental health problems who were in work fell steadily throughout the 1990s even when general rates of employment rose. They concluded:

> These data clearly show that, during the 1990s, the proportion of people with longer-term mental health problems in employment decreased substantially in Wandsworth. This decrease did not reflect general employment rates in the manner that might have been expected: employment rates among longer-term mental health service users fell when general

employment rates were falling, but continued to decrease when general employment rates rose again. This decrease did not reflect the national data on employment rates for disabled people more generally either, which remained constant at around 40% throughout the 1990s (Burchardt, 2000). It is likely that this difference reflects the greater discrimination experienced by people with mental health problems. (Perkins and Rinaldi, 2002, p 296)

Perkins and Rinaldi (2002) reported an employment rate of 19.7% among people with long-term mental health problems in 1990; this had fallen to only 8.1% in 1999. These rates are comparable with the reported rates for clients finding work quoted above.

For some of the clients, finding work may not necessarily be desirable. Although project managers were keen to encourage the association of project activities with 'work' and paid employment, some expressed concern about initiatives and schemes designed to assist people into paid employment, particularly when they were used for those with mental health problems. They reported that many of their clients who had mental health problems were not ready for employment and could suffer ill-effects if they were pushed into the workplace too early. They also expressed doubts about the ability of some of their clients to retain employment in the long term and of the use of employment statistics to measure the effectiveness of garden projects. Clients, too, expressed fears about going into the workplace, as this comment from a young man with mental health problems shows:

> **"Once my mood lifts some more, everything is hunky dory. I feel that I could do [...] I always feel that the grass is greener on the other side as a job, but the problem is I don't know what sort of job I would want, I don't know what sort of pressures would be put on me, I don't know what sort of people I'd be mixing with."** (Jim, project client, with mental ill health)

Although STH projects provide the opportunity for clients to engage in a regular activity that has some of the attributes of employment, it is not simply this routine that is valued or considered to be beneficial by the clients (and many of those involved in running the projects). The fact that gardening and horticultural activities take place outdoors in a 'natural' environment to which many clients develop an emotional attachment and the fact that the activities involve watching living plants grow is fundamental to the appeal and success of garden projects. This role of nature and the attraction of 'being outside' are examined on page 43. However, it is relevant to mention at this point, during the discussion of work and employment, that the nature of the work and the setting is important to the clients but this may occasionally be overlooked by project managers (and others) who are keen to focus on the similarities of project work and employment. In one particular example, a project manager reported in an interview that he considered it unimportant whether the clients were engaged in gardening or some form of manufacturing as long as they had ownership and control over the work:

> "To me, it doesn't matter whether we are making plastic windows, whether we're making components for cars, it is the *way* in which we do the work, and it is the *ownership* of that work, that *sense* of ownership of work that people need to have. And at the end of the day, the feel-good factor from work comes from when you have achieved something and you can see what you have achieved. And within horticulture, it is easy to see what you've achieved. You pot on a hundred plants, and they're neatly stacked in the greenhouse, in nice, neat order. At the end of the day, there is *something*, we've *achieved* that, there is a sense of achievement." (Tim, project organiser, project for people with mental ill health)

His colleague, also a member of staff, agreed with the notion that the exact nature of the work, that is, working in horticulture, was unimportant. The particular project was involved in growing mushrooms on a small commercial scale in a polytunnel that had controlled temperature, humidity and lighting. When the batch of mushroom culture was ready it was extremely productive and the mushrooms needed to be picked as soon as they appeared. Such a task could easily have been seen as repetitive and uninteresting. Yet, even under such intensive conditions it was viewed as nurture and cultivation and provided the clients with a sense of satisfaction because they had been party to the whole process of growing and harvesting:

> "... we have the mushroom cooperative, we see it right from the start, from the filling the tunnel with all the bags and, in my case, I come in and water the floors and do the temperatures at the weekend, so you see it right from the start right till you're picking, so it's your own product, what you've grown from the start six weeks previous, sort of thing, what you're picking, and then, you know, see the fruits of your labour, sort of thing." (Colin, project client, with mental ill health)

Cultivating mushrooms had been of such fascination to that particular interviewee that he had started to grow them at home.

Conclusion

There is some degree of ambivalence in the perception of project activities as *work*. It is clear that many clients (and some staff) do not see their activities as work because they do not feel under pressure to perform and also because gardening and other activities are enjoyable to them. They are activities that are also hobbies in many cases and for some project workers receiving a wage is almost a bonus, that is, "I'm being *paid* to do *this*". Some clients, however, like to think of themselves as *workers* as this elevates their status both in terms of self-perception and how they may be perceived by others. Receiving pay, however little, is an important part of this, and being able to call oneself a 'gardener' is a major step forward in self-esteem.

Whether project work is seen as work or not, those who attend projects on a regular basis derive the latent benefits normally associated with employment – structure, social contact and the other factors described above. Project work does not necessarily need to feel like employment to provide benefit, but for some the identification with work is clearly important. Equally important is the setting of the work in the natural environment, and the involvement of the work with the cultivation and nurture of living plants. These natural aspects are discussed on page 48.

Physical activity, health and well-being

There is a vast literature on the effects of physical activity and exercise on health (see Hardman and Stensel, 2003). Although these two terms are used synonymously, 'exercise' refers to physical activity that is planned, structured and carried out for the purpose of increasing or improving fitness while 'physical activity' can be incidental in the course of work or leisure.

Research has shown that increased physical activity is associated with a lower risk of cardiovascular and metabolic diseases (USDHHS, 1996) and may also be associated with a reduced risk of cancer (see Friedenreich, 2001). There is also strong evidence that a higher level of physical fitness is associated with a lower risk of mortality from all causes (Blair et al, 1995; Erikssen et al, 1998). Recent guidelines for the management of high blood pressure in general practice issued by the National Institute for Clinical Excellence (NEHGDG, 2004) also recommend an increase in physical exercise and review the available evidence suggesting a link between blood pressure and exercise. Lack of physical activity or exercise, on the other hand, are associated with poor physical health or disease, for example, obesity and diabetes – conditions that are presently causing particular concern among health professionals both in the UK and abroad.

Research suggests that the recent rise in the incidence of obesity is probably due more to a reduced level of physical activity than to increased food intake (Prentice and Jeb, 1995). Patterns of health and disease, however, are not evenly distributed throughout society. Research has shown that people with mental health problems and those with learning difficulties have poorer physical health than the rest of the population. For example, the mortality from natural causes, such as cardiovascular disease, is significantly increased in people from these two groups (see Brown, 1997; Harris and Barraclough, 1998). People with learning difficulties are almost four times more likely to die from cardiovascular disease than the rest of the population, and have a mortality due to respiratory disease, which may be up to 19 times higher (see Harris and Barraclough, 1998). While the increased mortality due to unnatural causes, such as accident and suicide, of people with mental ill health has received considerable attention, health problems caused by natural causes have aroused less interest, as Harris and Barraclough point out:

> **Death from natural causes is at least as important a source of the excess mortality in mental disorder as death from unnatural causes. The influences on death from natural causes probably vary more over time than those on unnatural causes. In the asylum era, for example, infectious disease resulting from overcrowding and poor nutrition was common. Today, with the most serious of mental disorders treated out of hospital, new influences may operate. (Harris and Barraclough, 1998, p 50)**

The factors influencing deaths from natural causes in these groups of people, therefore, may change with changing patterns of behaviour within society. It is possible that these groups of people may be at higher risk, for example, from the changing lifestyle and diet that have been blamed for the recent rise in obesity and diabetes. Brown (1997) has suggested that alcohol, smoking, an unhealthy diet and lack of exercise may be the factors driving excess natural cause mortality in schizophrenic patients. While evidence suggests that people with learning difficulties and mental health problems are at greater risk of developing diseases usually associated with poor diet and a lack of physical activity, it is highly likely that in many cases they are also unable to access facilities, such as sports and leisure centres, that are now popular for exercise and recreation.

One alternative to such indoor settings has been the creation of 'Green Gyms' offering people the opportunity to carry out physical activity in a natural environment and involving them in conservation work such as tree planting, hedge laying and habitat restoration. Recent evaluations of such projects have shown significant improvements in measures of cardiovascular fitness and indices of mental health (see Reynolds, 1999, 2002). There are presently around 50 Green Gyms active in the UK and although they are not intended specifically for vulnerable people such as those with mental health problems and learning difficulties, around 30% of users are unemployed (see Reynolds, 2002). While Green Gyms provide a relatively small number of places at present, garden projects offer many more clients the opportunity to work outside. Although these projects are not primarily intended to provide exercise facilities, they do, however, offer their clients the opportunity to engage in a regular, structured form of outdoor physical activity. Many of the tasks, such as digging or hard landscaping, require the exertion of substantial effort. Some of the conservation activities at garden projects are also similar to those found at the Green Gyms and while it could be argued as to whether these activities constitute physical activity or exercise, the clients interviewed invariably spoke of taking 'exercise' rather than engaging in 'physical activity'.

Many of the clients reported that they felt 'healthy' by working outside and in the 'fresh air', and, as discussed on page 46, 'fresh air' was synonymous with health. Clients acknowledged the link between physical activity or exercise and health. The following brief account, for example, is taken from an interview with a client who considered that the physical exertion on his allotment contributed to the reduction of his high blood pressure. Although there was no actual evidence that this was the case, the fact that the man believed that his work on the allotment was responsible for lowering his blood pressure encouraged him to continue participating at the project and engage in more physical activity:

"When I arrive in here in this country ... no speaking English ... I have blood pressure, I am really not very happy.... And really, this [plot] is now very healthy, because, I have blood pressure, help my blood pressure, I make exercises here, when I come to here, I

> arrive, believe me, all my problems going out, my brain working, my body working, I hope I working here, this is healthy." (Jindar, project client, for refugees and people with mental ill health)

There have been reports that observing plants can lower systolic blood pressure under laboratory conditions (Yamane et al, 2004), and Hartig et al (2003) reported that subjects walking in a nature reserve had lower blood pressure than those walking through an urban development. While these particular changes and differences may be attributable to physiological responses to altering conditions, rather than to changes in a pathological condition or disease state, it is possible that there is benefit to be derived from the environment in addition to that resulting from the activity or exercise.

A number of other specific examples of improvement in physical health were given by clients. In the case described by the client below, the project offered him the opportunity to engage in physical activity at his own pace, and without any pressure. The staff were supportive by ensuring that he did not exceed his physical capabilities. The variety of different activities available to him enabled him to choose ones that he felt did not overstretch him:

> "The key word with chronic fatigue syndrome, or ME, is pacing, you have to pace and build up slowly. Make sure you start at a level that you can manage and then increase it a little bit. That's the key thing for getting well from chronic [...]. Because if you've got ME you have to pace, and that's what I've been able [to do]. The staff understand that here. In fact, at the beginning, and still now, they still make sure I don't [...]. They say, 'Oh, well, you're doing too much here'.

> "So you can test yourself here slowly, slowly.

> "It's a very, very good environment to come and build up your energy levels." (Sam, project client, for people with physical or mental ill health)

When clients were asked how they thought their health had changed as a result of participating in a gardening project, 81% considered that it had improved (see Table 4.5). These responses were elicited by a semi-structured interview and not by using a specific health questionnaire. The SF-12 questionnaire (see Ware et al, 1995) was used in a pilot study, but even when the questions were read by the interviewers many clients found them ambiguous or difficult to answer and this approach was abandoned. It is important to point out that the sample of clients represented a great range of cognitive abilities and many had difficulties in communicating. For some, English was not their first language and this also caused difficulties.

Table 4.5: How do you think the project has affected your physical health?

	Frequency	%
Made no difference	18	16.1
Improved slightly	36	32.1
Improved a lot	55	49.1
Slightly worse	1	0.9
Don't know	2	1.8
Total	**112**	**100.0**

The one case where physical health had worsened was due to a fall at the project suffered by a woman who had had serious head injuries and had difficulties with balance and walking. Fifty-eight per cent of respondents who felt that their health had improved as result of attending the project gave a reason for this (see Table 4.6). The remainder were unable to provide a reason for their feeling of better health even when pressed by the interviewers; however, they did not change their view regarding the projects' effect on their health. Over a quarter of respondents felt 'fitter', and over a third reported reduced symptoms or reduced 'negative feelings' or emotions. Comments made to the interviewers included:

"I think it's helped stabilise my medical condition, as well. You know how medical conditions are influenced by social factors, too? And I think it's beneficial to people's physical health as well as to their mental well-being.

"... I've reduced my anticonvulsants." (Maureen, client with epilepsy, also reported fewer seizures since attending the project, two years)

"It's made me fitter – I've lost excess weight." (Thomas, project client, with mental ill health)

"I have more energy." (Andy project client, with mental ill health)

Table 4.6: Reasons given for perceived improvement of health

	Frequency	%
Feel better for fresh air	14	15.4
Feel fitter	24	26.4
Reduced symptoms or negative feelings	31	34.1
Increased motivation	2	2.2
No reason given	38	41.8

Note: Percentage of the 91 respondents who reported that their health had improved (either 'slightly' or 'a lot').

Mental health

Physical activity has been reported to improve mental health. Indeed, as described above, a study of Green Gyms showed improvement in indices of mental health (see Reynolds, 2002), and other published research suggests that physical exercise may be useful in the treatment of anxiety and depression (for a review see Burbach, 1997) and also Alzheimer's disease (Lindenmuth and Moose, 1990). Project organisers saw the improvement in the physical fitness of their clients as being linked to their emotional or psychological well-being and so encouraged physical activity. Many of the project volunteers who had experience of working with people with mental health problems in institutional settings spoke of the "dayroom culture of coffee and cigarettes" and little or no physical activity. The aim of projects, therefore, was to promote physical activity and so promote mental well-being and self-confidence, which, in some cases, could be transferred to activities outside the project:

> "It's about looking at increasing confidence, erm, becoming more physically fit. Because a lot of the problems with mental health is that people tend to sit around, smoke a lot, drink a lot of coffee and not do an awful lot else, you know. So, there's the physical side to it, getting outside, and then maybe giving people the confidence to try something like this at home. I mean, we have got some, a couple here that have got their own allotments now." (Arthur, tutor, project for people with mental ill health)

Forty-two per cent of all clients (and 33% of those with mental ill health) reported that they had taken up new hobbies or leisure activities at home as a result of attending the project. These were mostly gardening or horticultural activities, but a small number (5 to 6) reported a new interest in outdoor sports such as cycling and walking and 18 clients had taken up indoor, sedentary leisure activities, for example, computing or art.

As a result of attending the project, clients, themselves, also reported perceived improvements to their mental well-being, including feeling less depressed and anxious. Thirteen of the 49 clients with mental ill health said that their conditions had improved noticeably since starting at the project. Only four said that their project had made no difference to their health (either physical or mental). The remainder reported improvements in other areas of health and well-being including physical fitness, stamina and self-confidence. The physical activity and tasks of the project provided a distraction from the worries and troubles of some of the clients:

> "It is a good exercise, a good thing that we busy ourselves. When, I am upset or I am, I feel, something not good feeling, I came here, I forget everything, and I am happy, I feel. When I am coming here, I am happy and I work, and when I return to my house or my flat, I am also, I feel that I do something. Yeah. It is

important for everybody." (Hasan, client, project for refugees
and people with mental ill health)

While the client above appears to have been able to return home and feel
the continuing benefits of his activities, the following account from a client
with mental health problems shows the inherent tensions between the
distraction of the project and his continuing anxieties, although the project
does appear to give him something pleasurable to anticipate:

"Before I came here, as I said before, I was just severely
depressed and suicidal. I saw a psychologist and said that I
need to do something, because being sat at home with all this
nonsense going on in my mind isn't healthy. So I did, I eventually
came here. So, it takes me out of myself, it's a distraction from
what I, the things that are troubling me, although it never solves
anything, even the stuff that's going on in your mind, you never
really solve it, but it's a distraction.)

"You see, when I get home in the evenings, and weekends, it's
the same stuff going on in my head. But now, when I get home,
I can also think about things I've done at [the project] or any
problems that have come up here, and it is a distraction. I plan
what I'm going to do the next day, look forward to it. I always
look forward to coming." (Tony, project client, with mental ill
health)

It is interesting that gardening can act as such a distraction since many
gardening tasks are solitary and might seem to present an opportunity for
intrusive or worrying thoughts and anxieties. Project activities may also
be capable of attenuating some of the more serious symptoms of clients'
conditions. For example, the manager of a project for people with mental
health problems (particularly older people) reported that those of his
clients who experienced auditory hallucinations were able to cope better
by engaging in gardening activities:

"Especially people who are hearing voices. If they got mental
health problems and they're hearing voices. Erm. I've got quite a
few actually at the moment. And one of the problems they have
is able to take the mind off their voices.

"Now it's been, it's been, oh, quite a few occasions, clients have
actually said to me, it's one of the few activities they do, where
they're able to do this, they can do other activities, like pottery
or art or walking or what have you, and they find it very difficult
for their, the voices to stop interfering with their thoughts.
With horticulture, it's, they're enjoying it so much and it's so
concentrating on what they're doing that they find that the
voice problem sort of goes in the background." (Stuart, project
organiser, project for people with mental ill health)

"And I've had also a chappie who used to physically run, the voices would be in his mind. And he, he would run away from the voices. But, he actually came to gardening, he said exactly the same thing. Gardening takes my mind off the voices." (Stuart, project organiser, project for people with mental ill health)

Similarly, a young man, interviewed by the researchers, also reported that his auditory hallucinations stopped when he was involved in gardening. The only other activity that did the same for him was riding his motorcycle. While these two activities require different degrees of concentration, care and skill, they would appear to have similar capacities for providing distraction. It is possible that the common factor in this particular case is the exposure to the external environment. It is equally possible that these two activities are simply ones that he enjoyed and found absorbing. Various forms of distraction techniques have been used as part of cognitive-behaviour therapy (CBT) in the treatment of psychotic patients who experience auditory hallucinations despite drug treatment (see Haddock et al, 1998). These have included the use of personal stereos, reading aloud, mental arithmetic and mental games and 'activity scheduling', that is, identifying and emphasising those tasks that appear to cause a reduction in the severity of symptoms – a technique that is also used with depressed patients (see Williams, 1992).

Distraction, as part of a CBT therapy programme, has been found to be effective in reducing the severity of auditory hallucinations; however, the effect is variable and is not maintained at follow-up after the treatment. Some researchers have also failed to observe an effect (see Haddock et al, 1998). It is possible that for some individuals gardening and other project activities form part of an informal process of activity scheduling – clients seek out those particular tasks and surroundings that make them feel better. The emphasis on choice and variety by project staff, some of whom have received training in CBT, may help to facilitate that process. If the activities do reduce any of the clients' symptoms then there is an incentive for them to continue attending the project. The pattern of attendance at garden projects is one of regular, long-term participation.

Seventy-four clients (54%) listed outdoor sports and recreation as their hobbies. These included gardening, mountain biking, hill walking, swimming and so on. For them projects may represent an additional or supplementary source of exercise. However, 35 clients (26%) listed only indoor or sedentary activities and 29 (21%) reported that they had no outside interests beyond the project. For the last two groups projects may represent the only source of meaningful activity (and hence distraction) and the only opportunity for physical activity or exercise in a structured environment. The following quote is taken from an interview with a man with learning difficulties who attended a horticulture and woodwork training programme at a city farm:

"We wouldn't have been able to do anything, if we wouldn't have come on these [courses].

"No. We would have sat looking at four ... the four walls.

"Like, four. Better than looking at four walls." (Mike, client with learning difficulties)

The social aspects of projects and contact with other clients and staff were listed as being key factors in reducing clients' feelings of depression and anxiety and providing enjoyment. For many clients, projects were the only point of social contact and this dimension of garden projects is discussed on page 52.

Conclusion

The observations described here are based on subjective self-assessments made by clients themselves. They show that clients felt better in themselves when attending projects and attributed this to their participation. Garden projects offer clients an opportunity to engage in physical activity. This is both valued and enjoyed, and may be especially important as many of the clients are from groups that are at greater risk than the general population of developing serious illnesses, such as cardiovascular disease, which may be prevented or attenuated by higher levels of physical activity. Outdoor physical activity is also perceived to be 'healthy' and clients reported feeling both healthier and fitter as a result of participation, although no physical measurements or recordings were taken.

Development of self-confidence and self-esteem

The development of self-confidence and self-esteem is a recurrent and important theme in research on STH and associated research into the beneficial effects of exposure to nature or wilderness. Self-esteem refers to a general feeling of self-worth or self-value, while self-confidence is the feeling that an individual is likely to succeed in a task and has few hesitations or reservations about attempting it. These two dimensions of self-concept are interrelated and are also often conflated.

There are scales and instruments for measuring self-esteem. For example, Rosenberg's (1965) 10-item measure of self-esteem has been widely used in research in this field. However, changes in individuals' perceptions of their own self-confidence and self-esteem are frequently self-reported or emerge during in-depth interviews, or are recorded by other types of questionnaire.

Hyer et al (1996) examined the effects of Outward Bound programmes on a group of US war veterans suffering from combat-related post-traumatic stress disorder (PTSD). Although they found no discernible effects on a range of objective measures of the symptoms of their patients, they reported that their patients found the experience to be valuable in building self-esteem and self-confidence (as perceived by the clients themselves and reported during interviews). They suggested that the battery of instruments that they used was not able to measure the specific impact of the outdoor programme that led to the effects recorded during interviews.

While scales of self-confidence and self-esteem are undoubtedly useful, they do have limitations, for example, when used with people who have difficulties in communicating or who have low motivation. In-depth interviews and simplified questionnaires can then be particularly useful in exploring changes in perceived self-confidence. For example, Seller et al (1999) observed that increased self-confidence was one of four main areas reported by the participants of an allotment-based group for people with mental health problems. They used a questionnaire to investigate their patients' responses, although they did not use a formal measure of self-esteem, such as Rosenberg's scale. In an extension of this work, Fieldhouse (2003) explored themes from in-depth interviews and observed that the participants reported "new perspectives of their own abilities", which prompted them to revise their views of their own capabilities. In other words their own confidence in their abilities had been enhanced by attending the group. Other published accounts of increased self-confidence include those of Wichrowski et al (1998) and Strauss and Gabaldo (1998) who reported increased self-confidence in their case histories of stroke patients participating in horticultural therapy.

In our study issues regarding self-esteem were examined in relation to work. Clients reported that participating at garden projects increased their sense of status and worth and made them feel like 'workers' or 'gardeners' (see pages 71-2) and the receipt of pay further enhanced this feeling of self-worth. Clients whose roles included helping other clients, for example, where there were mixed disability groups, spoke of feeling "happy" and at being able to help others less able than themselves. This engendered a sense of usefulness and purpose that contrasted with feelings of being "worthless" prior to joining the project. Feelings of self-worth were also expressed by clients in relation to simply attending the project and taking part in something useful rather than staying at home and being inactive. For example:

> "My whole sense of self-esteem was very, very low, very, very low. I didn't think a lot of myself, or others, I mean, I didn't really care about others, I just cared about myself. And so coming here has [...] it was a bit of a long slog to, actually, sort of, get myself out of the pattern that I'd got myself into. It was quite repetitive, sort of, just staying indoors all the time. But once I did get there, it was so beneficial, it's unbelievable. My whole mood has lifted. It's, erm, I just love it. Even if it's raining, I love being out there." (Neil, project client, with mental ill health)

Case history: Laura

Laura is 46. She suffered brain damage at birth and has severe learning difficulties, with limited verbal capacity. She lives at home with her mother, who cares for her. Laura attended a day care centre for many years until two years ago when she joined the gardening project.

Laura's mother said that Laura was unhappy and not making any progress at the day care centre (for people with learning difficulties and challenging behaviour). Laura's mother said, "[Laura needed to be] with a group of more able people and a less frenetic, noisy group than at the [day care centre] where I think she was quite disturbed".

The gardening project organiser added, "[Laura] didn't like being put in with people that had severe behavioural problems who were very noisy. She hated that noise. She really struggles with that".

Since moving to the gardening project Laura's mother and project staff have noticed an improvement both in Laura's confidence and her skills.

The project organiser explained, "Laura has problems expressing herself, and in holding things and doing things easily, because she's got motor problems with her hands, her grip. And, she's, actually, since [she moved here] her ability to speak up for herself, her self-advocacy skills have grown enormously. She's asking to do things in the greenhouse, and providing they're not too tiny a thing, she can do them. She's been out there with the hoe, when everybody else is digging she had the hoe, and was hoeing and was singing away. Her whole demeanour, it's her whole demeanour, it's her mental health, her physical health, her abilities have all grown within the last year, vastly. The parents and carers have all commented on the difference".

Laura's mother added, "Laura is very happy with the group. When a gardening project was first suggested I really thought there would be nothing within her capabilities ... but she does fill pots with compost, sorts labels. She can recognise pictures so she can sort out different flowers and she has become much more independent".

"She's also become more independent at home also, and much more chatty, she joins in conversation more. She can string together more than three words, she matches things in her mind. She will instigate conversation now which she never did before. Her conversation has improved. She talks to me now in longer sentences and speaks on the telephone to my friends which she never did before."

"For Laura gardening is ... she wouldn't gain anything from other skills projects. She talks about gardening and the atmosphere at the project is something she can relate to and now she watches gardening programmes on TV – she's quite a follower of Alan Titchmarsh now – and we can talk about gardening and the programmes too. Gardening is a very relaxing, gentle process, or it can be and the way they organise it at the project works very well – the ones who can do the heavier, contract work but that wouldn't suit Laura – she enjoys being down there [on site]. It's definitely benefited her. It gives her a purpose and I think she feels quite valued as a member of the group. This is of course partly to do with the particular staff they have down there, she interacts with them very well."

Perceptions of confidence revolved around the ability to perform tasks successfully (or competently), to learn new skills and to attempt (and succeed) at activities which, at first sight, may have appeared difficult or daunting. Projects aimed to build confidence in their clients through facilitating success in gardening (and other) tasks, demonstrating to them that they could succeed. Project organisers promoted training (including in some cases accredited training leading to formal qualifications) and the development of skills while offering increasing levels of responsibility through involvement with different aspects of the project, such as helping with the sale of produce at a farmers' market. One project organiser summed up the aims of his project as follows:

> "I think confidence really, it's increasing their confidence and belief in themselves. I think in general if you're looking at the group as a whole, that's probably the biggest thing.
>
> "It happens naturally and always has done, but I think it's just, it's also boosted by the way that we're looking to increase people's responsibilities, gradually picking up on their skills and using them to give them more responsibility here within [the project]. And also if they're enthusiastic, then finding opportunities for them to get involved in, like, the farmers' market and weekend events, that sort of thing, really, volunteering." (Andy, volunteer, project for people with learning difficulties)

Ninety-four per cent of clients (out of 107 respondents to the question) said that they had learned new skills at the project. Unsurprisingly, the most frequently reported new skills in this group were those related to gardening (90%). However, many also reported that they had learned social skills (53%) and IT and administrative skills (23%). A small number reported that they had acquired literacy (9%), numeracy (8%) and team-working (7%) skills. Such skills were not only useful at the project; they were also transferable to other situations such as the home. For example, IT skills enabled clients to use e-mail and the Internet at home and new gardening skills and knowledge enabled clients to tackle their own gardens when previously they had neither the skills nor possibly the inclination to do so:

> "The projects affect me, it's not affected, it's helped me.
>
> "When I started in the garden, at the same time, I started gardening in my home as well. Otherwise, I didn't bother my garden.
>
> "So, [...] helped me to do the gard- how, however, how they do it over there. And at the same time, I can do it at home and use my skills here, at home as well." (Parvin, client, project for women from minority ethnic groups)

The acquisition of social skills (and in many cases reacquisition of them) and the introduction to social opportunities also led to increases in perceived self-confidence. Many clients reported that they had few social contacts prior to attending the project and some had lost the ability to interact socially. Garden projects enabled clients to work together and to interact (if they wished). They enabled clients to increase their self-confidence in social interaction, not only while they were at the project but also in other spheres of their lives, although the extent of social contact outside the project was often limited. The social dimension of gardening projects is discussed on page 52.

It was not just the acquisition of skills that appeared to increase self-confidence but also the experience of success in the garden environment. Garden activities, such as sowing seeds or weeding, provided tangible results that led to a sense of satisfaction and achievement. A point frequently made by project staff was that the horticultural knowledge and experience of staff was particularly important because it enabled them to ensure that clients' activities were successful. The following quote taken from an interview with a client with mental health problems shows his sense of achievement and confidence from the results of his efforts:

> "Well, I mean, I guess the most I've gained from being here is, after my release from hospital, I was feeling very low in confidence and self-esteem. I was very withdrawn, and painfully shy, as well, and since coming here, and people being kind and compassionate towards me, erm, I've been able to build up my confidence again, and felt more self-worth, as well, from being able to see results from my work.

> "Well, even if it's just planting a seed and seeing a flower grow, you know, it's a sense of achievement. You feel like you've made a bit of a difference." (John, project client, with mental ill health)

Facilitation of self-confidence by positive feedback to the clients was also used by the project staff. The clients' sense of self-confidence was reinforced by praise and encouragement delivered by the staff in the event of even minor achievements, as these two examples show:

> "They can actually achieve things in the horticulture and the agriculture and the workshop units. And for the first time in their lives they actually feel valued as well because we always praise, even small milestones we always praise, and I think they feel very valued here." (Fiona, volunteer, training project for mixed ability groups)

> "And then, they know themselves when they've got it, as well, because, erm, that sense of achievement is, you know, you give them appropriate praise and encouragement for it, and it's like a rolling stone, the more praise and encouragement you give them, the more confident they become, and so they move on to the next skill, they've learned that skill, they move on to the next one." (Sue, volunteer, project for people with learning difficulties, mental ill health and other disabilities)

Project staff also encouraged and promoted team work in order to boost self-confidence, particularly when it involved a difficult task that required a combined effort. Such a job could be used as an opportunity to demonstrate to the clients that what appeared to be a seemingly impossible task could be achieved. In other words, that they had the capabilities to achieve more than they realised, especially if their previous experience of the care services had led them to believe that their abilities were limited or their activities should be curtailed:

> "... like that big rock that was sitting near here, that took eight of us to move from the back field.

> "And it was like, 'Oh, we can't do that, it's impossible to move that', and you say, 'Yeah, we can, we'll try it', and it's just the idea that you can try something, and if you put your mind to it, and you put your energy into it, you can do it.

> "The people who just like to get focused on something, really heavy work, the impossibility of it: 'Oh, can we put that, can we stand that piece of wood up, here? Let's do it, let's try it'. You know, trying something difficult, that looks difficult or impossible. These people have been told for years, 'Oh, you're ill, you can't do that'." (Adam, volunteer, project for people with mental ill health)

Overall, 45% of clients (out of 106 respondents to the question) considered that they had 'quite a lot' or a 'lot' of confidence in themselves. Thirty per cent replied that they had 'some' confidence, while only 17% felt that they had 'none' or 'very little' confidence in themselves. The majority of clients (80%) felt that they had the confidence to speak out about matters they considered important and 84% thought that their self-confidence had increased in some measure as a result of attending the project.

Political engagement

Over half of clients (54.5%) felt that they 'had a say' in how the project was run. Different projects had different systems and processes for engaging clients in the management of the project. Formal meetings were a feature of many of the larger projects; these were held monthly or bimonthly and the purpose was to look at planned project activities and overall performance of the project. Attendance at such meetings was voluntary but very few chose not to participate. The experience was valued and considered by some clients to be a way of promoting equality among project participants – clients and staff alike. Such democratisation of project management was also the intention of some project workers:

> "... we have a site meeting here every week and try to get trainees, that's myself, and other trainees, involved. They do, they definitely do that, the staff do that, that's the focus here.

So I think that's very important, and you're encouraged to take on responsibility, you know, you're encouraged in many, many ways, so that's very important too, I think." (Sam, project client, with mental ill health)

"I like to feel needed myself, and obviously they do, and it's nice to be able to see each person knowing a little bit about different things and then when the meetings come up everyone puts it together; and we take in turns to chair the meetings, which gives people a little bit more responsibility, a chance to discuss things and put things forward, which I think is really good because it gives a kind of a level, a one sort of level for everyone, because each person is contributing in some sort of way, whether it be knowledge or work or whatever." (Kevin, project client, with mental ill health)

Around 31% of all clients who answered the question reported that they would like more of a say in the running of the project and 28% of those who felt they already had a say in how their project was run wanted to have an increased input. So, although projects actively seek to engage their clients in decision making, a number of clients would still like an increased role in the running of their project.

Creativity and confidence

Arts and craft activities formed an integral part of many projects, and 19% of projects had dedicated craft workshops, while others practised arts and craft activities, either in the open air or in buildings and shelters, which often doubled up for other uses, for example, storage sheds or classrooms and tea rooms. Often natural materials were used in the artwork, and these provided the link between the garden and horticultural activities and arts and crafts, for example, locally grown willow and dogwood were used in sculpture and weaving. Similarly, sculptures and mosaics were used to decorate the project site or garden. The impact on self-confidence (and self-esteem) arose from both the learning of new skills and from the sense of satisfaction of creating something new. Clients were often pleased with their efforts and keen to show off their arts and craft work and often asked for it to be photographed or requested that they be photographed with their creations. Many of the arts and craft activities offered by projects had not previously been attempted by clients, and project organisers were keen for them to have a go so that they could see that success was possible:

"... some people may never have had any confidence so, actually, even just trying to get people to see that they can almost do anything, given the opportunity, and hence the blacksmithing and the crafts that, you know, some people might never have, you know, attempted anything like that in their lives." (Phil, project organiser, project for people with mental ill health)

The following quotes, from an interview with a client with mental health problems, shows that acquiring skill in a new and unpractised area could be effective in generating a feeling of self-confidence:

> **"Well, we've done some willow sculptures, we've made chairs out of willow trees. We've made a big, sort of, arch out of willow trees. This other guy made a wasp out of willow trees, it had eyes and a body and a tail.**
>
> **"It's difficult at first but once you've laid down the foundations and, you know, the weaving is actually quite easy, it just takes a lot of time, you know, but I think the hardest thing about it is actually planning where to put in the foundations into the garden, you know.**
>
> **Well, I think it's helped my confidence and, it's also, it's, I mean, I'd never done, I wouldn't know where to start about whether sculptures, I mean, I still wouldn't, now, because I'm not actually experienced at doing it, but I can do the weaving, and, I can do digging and stuff, and pulling down fences, so I can do all the basic things, really." (Matthew, project client, with mental ill health)**

Clients who tried activities that they were not familiar with were often surprised both by their success in those activities and their enjoyment of them. This sometimes led to a deeper interest. In the case below the client discovered his aptitude at woodcarving after being introduced to it at a project. He has subsequently followed it up with the intention of being self-employed as a woodcarver and woodworker:

> **"And then I started to get into the wood and, you know, and started carving for the first time. I'd never tried it before. I'd done woodwork at school, but I just fell in love with it, I just loved working with wood, so I've sort of gone off from there on to, you know, making furniture and rocking horses, walking sticks, chainsaw carvings." (Maurice, project client, with mental ill health**

Confidence and relationships

Over half of the clients (54%) thought that a gardening project had improved their relationship with their family (either 'slightly' or 'a lot') and 43% of clients reported that the project had improved their relationships with friends (see Tables 4.7 and 4.8). No clients replied that their relationships appeared to have worsened as a result of participation in a project. Both increased self-confidence and increased self-esteem were given as reasons for the improved relationships (see Table 4.9). Additionally, clients reported that the newly acquired skills and knowledge gave them

Table 4.7: The effect of attending a project on the relationship with family

	Number of respondents	%
Made no difference	45	43.3
Improved slightly	30	28.8
Improved a lot	24	23.1
Don't know	5	4.8
Total	**104**	**100.0**

Table 4.8: The effect of attending a project on the relationship with friends

	Number of respondents	%
Made no difference	46	45.5
Improved slightly	30	29.7
Improved a lot	13	12.9
Don't know	12	11.9
Total	**101**	**100.0**

"something to talk about" with their family and friends. Where their family members or friends were interested in gardening they were able to share in that interest and participate in conversation. But also simply having experienced something new, which they found interesting, gave clients material to relate to their family, friends and acquaintances. As the mother of a client explained:

> "Well, he just tells you what he's been doing and what he, you know, more or less, basically, tells you what he's done. And then when my daughter-in-law comes, or my son comes, he tells them. So, he always lets you know what he's been doing.
>
> "He always talks about what he, he always tells you what he's done. I mean, obviously, more here, because there's more involved here. Because he worked at [a supermarket] for nine years, erm, just pushing trolleys." (Mother of client with learning difficulties and physical disabilities)

Table 4.9: Reasons given for improved relationships with family and friends

	Number of respondents
Increased self-confidence	23
Increased self-esteem	14
Shared interest – "something to talk about"	18
Shared interest – actual involvement of family and friends with project activity	5

Project workers also recognised the value of having material for conversation and the effect that that had on clients' feelings of self-esteem, as the following quote illustrates:

"... the quality of his life has improved a hundred-fold since he's been coming here, erm, from a guy who walked on two sticks and was just going to the therapeutic bit because there was nothing else for him to do. He now has the responsibility again. He's, it is, it's the work ethic, isn't it? Because when you go to the pub, what do you talk about? You talk about your job, you talk about the day you've had, and it's all self-worth, the self-worth thing." (Project organiser speaking about a client recovering from a stroke)

Conclusion

Issues regarding self-confidence and self-esteem were usually combined both by project organisers and by clients. However, it was possible to separate the feelings of self-worth (that is, self-esteem) from those of self-confidence. Perceptions of self-esteem and self-worth were apparent, for example, as a result of the status gained from being a project participant and hence a gardener or worker. This was especially so if the work was remunerated. Self-confidence was seen as the willingness of clients to undertake many different activities, including arts and crafts, and their sense of competence in those tasks. Also, by the satisfaction they appeared to experience in creating objects of arts and craft and by acquiring, and possessing, the necessary skills for those tasks. This success was understood by (most) clients and recognised and interpreted as a feeling of confidence in their abilities and reported as such in interviews and in responses to the questionnaires. Project staff actively sought to increase the self-confidence of their clients by a variety of means, including positive feedback, increasing their level of responsibility, facilitating their work to ensure that clients succeeded, demonstrating that major tasks were achievable, teaching new skills and giving opportunities to try different activities which could result in specific abilities or talents being discovered.

The confidence gained, through the acquisition of skills and knowledge, also appeared to have a positive effect on some clients' relationships with their families and friends.

The involvement of vulnerable clients in the research process

Photographic participation and elicitation study

Three STH projects for people with learning difficulties were approached to participate in the photographic participation and elicitation study. This part of the study was introduced in order to involve particularly vulnerable groups in research more effectively and to promote sensory approaches that did not rely heavily on verbal capacity.

The three projects were chosen from the 24 STH projects included in the research to look in more detail at their work practices and client involvement in STH. The aims of the photographic study were explained to project organisers who then discussed these with their clients. Both clients and organisers from the three projects agreed to participate in the study.

Not all clients (with learning difficulties) at these projects took part in the photographic study, only those who expressed an interest in it. Further, one of the three projects that had agreed to take part initially decided against participation at a later date. Thus, photographic data was collected from two projects. Disposable (24 exposure) cameras were given to 19 participants with learning difficulties, 10 at one project (all male) and nine at the other (five male, four female).

These clients were asked to take photographs on site at projects over a period of time (approximately one month). General guidance to clients included asking them to take photographs of aspects of their attendance at projects that they particularly enjoyed or liked. The research team revisited the projects after a month to collect the cameras and to discuss progress with project organisers and clients who participated in the study.

A content analysis was conducted of all of the images generated (471 in total) in this part of the study, and a separate analysis of clients' favourite photographs was carried out. Categories and sub-categories were used to indicate the subject matter of the photographs. These included:

- indoor and outdoor gardening activity;
- indoor and outdoor social activity (posed and non-posed pictures of other clients or project organisers);
- plants: seedlings, cuttings, raised beds and borders;
- inside structures such as greenhouses and polytunnels;
- contract work;
- tools;
- transport;
- structures such as sheds and greenhouses;
- general project site.

While the 'other' category makes up the largest percentage in respect of photographic content, it is important to note that this category included a number of sub-categories such as 'general views on and off site', 'completed work', 'specific tasks', 'visits', mixed category images, and also included those images that were indistinct or blurred. While the use of categories provides a picture of the types of activity clients were engaged in at projects, as well as the significance of various themes in respect of the content of the photographic images, in one or two cases it was difficult to categorise absolutely the main subject matter of the images and sometimes the clients were unable to indicate this themselves.

Combining the 'indoor', 'outdoor', 'other clients' and 'project staff' categories in respect of photographs of *people* at projects (posed and non-posed), these comprise the largest percentage (42.7%) of images taken by clients (see Table 4.10). This figure emphasises the significance of social activity and relationships at projects even for those groups with cognitive and communication impairments (many of whom do not make, or have the opportunity of making, close friendships in their daily lives) and, interestingly, reflects the findings in the overall study of 24 projects.

Only 17% of photographs taken by clients were 'problematic' in some way (and only 2.7% were blurred and thus unable to be analysed). Of this 17%, 7.2% were taken at an angle/upside down, a further 7.2% had an object (usually a thumb) obscuring some or most of the image, and 2.7% were blurred, dark or indistinct.

Photographic elicitation

It was intended that the photographic participation study would also include photographic elicitation techniques, that is, participants in the study were asked to comment on the significance or importance of

Table 4.10: Content analysis of photographic images taken by clients at projects

Photo content	%
Outdoor client activity and posed	19.5
Plants (indoor and outdoor)	16.7
Indoor client activity and posed	13.5
Other clients taking photographs	7.8
Tools	5.7
Structures	4.4
Contract work	3.8
Transport	2.7
Project staff	1.9
Other	24.0

Note: Total number of clients = 19, total number of photographs = 471.

the photographs they had taken and to choose five of their 'favourites'. Depending on the severity of clients' learning difficulties, eliciting verbal responses was not always possible, and indeed, the intention of the photographic study was to avoid over-reliance on verbal responses. However, most clients were able to indicate 'favourite images' even if they were unable to express verbally the reasons for their choice.

All clients were asked to choose five favourite photographs and, where possible, to explain their reasons for their choices. Fourteen out of the 19 participants in the study were able to either choose their favourites and give reasons for their choice or indicate by pointing to the images they liked the most. Five participants simply did not have the verbal capacity to explain or engage in discussion or activity about their favourite images. Across the two projects, 14 participants selected a total of 68 images as 'favourite' pictures. These were categorised as follows:

Table 4.11: Clients' favourite images

Subject	Number of photographs	%
People	31	45.5
Plants	18	26.4
Tools	5	7.3
General site	3	4.4
Visit	3	4.4
Completed work	2	2.9
Structures	2	2.9
Contract work	2	2.9
Transport	2	2.9

Discussion

It is interesting that the findings from this photographic participation and elicitation study reflect so closely the findings of the overall investigation with regard to people and plants. The social benefits to clients of STH are significant in terms of the findings from the study as a whole. Further, being outside, the natural environment and connectedness with nature are also important aspects in respect of most clients' experiences of STH. However, it could not be assumed that clients who are particularly vulnerable, for example, those with severe learning difficulties, experience and benefit from STH in the same way as other clients for a number of reasons. First, people with severe learning difficulties can often be disempowered by health and social care systems or institutions that are not always intended to foster independence or help build social networks for clients.

Many project organisers talked about their clients' lives outside the gardening projects – especially where clients with learning difficulties were attending day care facilities or had been placed in residential institutions – as restricted, highly routinised and marginalised. Clients in these situations would rarely socialise with new people, were not visible in local communities and had few opportunities to develop independence or personal skills.

One of the project organisers explained,

> **"I see our role as very important; that we're, I'm not sure whether integration is quite the right word, but we're demonstrating, actively demonstrating, that people with learning disabilities have a valuable contribution to make. We're showing that they can work alongside able-bodied people. And it's good for our volunteers because it brings them into contact with a wider number of people; and also for those other outside people. They may have never encountered, and certainly not worked with people with learning disabilities, and they see these people – you know, they're eager, they're willing, they put a lot of hard physical work in – and, as I say, that's what I see as one of the most important things that we do, is to show people that people with learning disabilities are, should be, valued members of the community. They have something to contribute."**

Second, people with learning difficulties sometimes lack the self-esteem that may enable them to participate in team work and activities with people they do not know well. Furthermore, they often require dedicated help and support to assist them in making new friends or undertaking tasks that are new to them. Such is the nature of work at STH projects that clients often have to work together in teams and undertake physically demanding tasks or jobs that require concentration. Sometimes, clients are encouraged to participate in such tasks gradually over many months and dedicated staff are always available to lend support. However, at other times clients are allowed degrees of freedom in terms of what they undertake and who they work with in order to help foster independence and allow friendships to develop.

The success of projects in effectively supporting people with learning difficulties in these ways is reflected in the findings from the photographic participation and elicitation study. The evidence here points absolutely to the importance of *social* and therapeutic *horticulture* to clients who are particularly vulnerable. The fact that in both the general content analysis of photographs and in the analysis of clients' favourite images, both sets of data point to the importance of 'people and plants' suggests that these are significant factors in terms of the benefits to these clients of attending STH projects.

However, there is a danger in assuming a depth of meaning here as the participants in this part of the study were unable to expand verbally on the meaningfulness or significance of the images they chose as favourites. Thus, it would be difficult to analyse these findings in the same way the overall findings are analysed and discussed. For example, many of the participants in the photographic study took pictures of plants and green spaces. However, this does not mean that 'sense of place' has inevitable significance for them in respect of an emotional attachment to the physical space of the gardening project, as we describe on pages 50-1, because these clients were unable to verbalise their experiences, and only visualise them through the use of photographs. Even in those cases where participants were able to choose and talk about their favourite photographs, in many instances they simply described the picture itself. For example, "That's my friend Laura", or, "That's the day we got the chipper".

However, it was clear from what some of the participants said about their favourite photographs that they held some significance for them, particularly in terms of their friendships, engaging in team work or successfully undertaking a rewarding task, as the following photographs and quotations illustrate:

Photograph taken by Robert of his friend Phillip. Robert is laughing when he says he took the picture of Phillip, "because he doesn't like having his photograph taken and I caught him between the Portakabins".

"That's on contract work. I like contract work." (Ted)

"We cut it down and I liked it. We had a fire, I like having fires." (Carl)

The success of the method: presentation or interpretation

If participants in research cannot tell us but are able to show us their experiences through, in this case, the use of participative photography, then it would seem appropriate to some extent to allow the images to 'speak for themselves', rather than over-emphasise the need to interpret or analyse, which is why we do not want to try and do that here.

The intention of this photographic participation and elicitation study was to emphasise the visual, rather than the verbal, capacity of clients with particular vulnerabilities. In which case, it matters less that the clients with learning difficulties who took part in this phase of the study did not talk in any detail about their photographs and more that they took part in the research process more effectively.

Furthermore, this approach is far more congruent with the inclusive aspect of the study and allows us to move away from not only a heavy reliance on the verbal skills of those participants who have impaired verbal communication capacity, but also an over-strict reliance on interpretation by the researchers themselves. Such interpretation or *amanuensis* (Booth, 1996) can mean that researchers, however unwittingly, are drawn into "betraying their subjects by representing them" (Booth, 1996, p 243). We wish to discuss issues of presentation and interpretation further in this section.

Presentation

Booth has argued:

> **Textbook methods of social research discriminate against
> people with learning difficulties. Methods that rely on reading or
> writing or abstract reasoning or verbal fluency may effectively
> exclude them from the role of respondent or informant in ways
> that mirror their exclusion from wider society. Wittingly or
> unwittingly the use of these methods also helps to reinforce
> the medical model of learning difficulties as individual deficits.
> (Booth, 1996, p 252)**

The use of photographic participation and elicitation methods in this study
has been successful both in terms of providing an antidote to a strictly
medical perspective, and in including participants with serious learning
difficulties in research more effectively. Its success can be further measured
in terms of the participants who used photography at STH projects and
the volunteers who witnessed clients' participation; both groups not
only recognised the usefulness of the photographic method as a more
appropriate research tool, but also enjoyed the act of photography itself
and the opportunity to demonstrate visually the STH experience.

However, in respect of providing evidence that is not only worthwhile to
research participants, but also has value and credibility in the broader
contexts of academia and political structures, then we have to look
more carefully at the usefulness of photography. For researchers, there
are undeniable pressures and conflicts outside the process of conducting
research itself that mean they must somehow reconcile tensions between
the demands of, for example, academia, scientific communities, the funders
of research and political structures (policy makers and so on) and between
the need to be faithful to a participatory philosophy that promotes the
interests, experiences and needs of the subjects of, or participants in,
research studies.

The inherent difficulty in attempting to reconcile these tensions lies in
the fact that conventional and 'scientific' research methods have tended
to have more credibility than less conventional, user-led approaches.
And yet more orthodox or recognised methods (for example, surveys,
questionnaires, health and well-being scales) do not always work
effectively with vulnerable groups such as those with learning difficulties.
Furthermore, these groups (and perhaps for this very reason) have often
either been left out of research studies altogether or, as Booth has said,
"have mostly been treated as objects of study rather than credited with
any integrity as people" (1996, p 238). More recently there has been an
increasing interest in presenting human, lived experience in research that,
as Booth has also recognised, can "restore [the] emotional content of
human experience" (Booth, 1996, p 237).

It is clear that a key objective of research studies, which include particularly vulnerable groups (and especially those who do not have the cognitive or communicative capacity to participate in research studies using conventional methods), is to provide evidence of meaningfulness for these groups – to allow insight into their 'inner world'. The methods we use in this respect must then be faithful not in representing or interpreting experience but in presenting or illustrating it. Photographic participation in this sense seems to be a more appropriate device to achieve this objective.

Furthermore, if, as Bowker (1993, p 28), has argued, "No faithful method of retrieving biographical truth exists", we must conclude that there are degrees of faithfulness only and that photographic participation methods here are closer to the faithful presentation of lived experience (of, in this case, people with learning difficulties) than other methods that rely on either second-hand accounts or on interpretation. The success or effectiveness of the photographic method in this study can be measured both in respect of the extent of participants' involvement in, and enjoyment of, this part of the study as well as in the amount and content of the data produced (discussed earlier).

The success of photography here can be further understood in terms of its combination of the visual and the personal. The photographs command the viewer's attention and, as the photographs have been taken by the participants themselves, they are also absorbing in a personal sense in that they provide direct insight into the experiences of those participants who have taken the pictures in the first place.

Interpretation

Booth (1996) argues that standard tests such as, for example, reliability and validity "are neither appropriate nor adequate when lives are not consistent, biographical truth is a will-o'-the-wisp and stories inevitably reflect something of the teller" (p 253). In this sense, photographic participation and elicitation approaches are similar to less conventional, but perhaps more appropriate research methods that include vulnerable participants in research studies more effectively, for example, narrative research techniques in which stories are told about subjects (in particular people with learning difficulties) based on their experiences. The role of the narrative researcher is to 'piece together' what participants say to tell (arresting) stories. However, even this method, unlike photography, inevitably relies on interpretation in a way that presenting pictures taken by participants themselves does not, especially if photographs are presented in such a way as to be able to 'speak for themselves' (that is, without the need for analysis or over-interpretation by researchers).

However, the challenge of the photographic method lies in reconciling the need for faithful demonstration or presentation and the need to inform wider audiences. Simply presenting the photographs on their own would be useful in that it would allow audiences or viewers a glimpse into the inner world and experiences of vulnerable groups they would otherwise know little about (and without the influencing 'voice' of the researcher). Sometimes, visual research relies simply on presentation and audience participation. For example, in describing his home movie project, Raine (1994, p 6) has said, "I don't want people to worry about whether it's true or whether it's fiction, I just want them to kind of live in this work – enter it, exist in it, enjoy it".

Other visual research has also promoted this intention. Farrell's pictorial evidence collected in the form of artwork from people with Aphasia is a further example here (see Carr, 2002). Aside from written contextual information, the participants' artwork is presented on its own to demonstrate their direct experiences of living with Aphasia. Where viewers or audiences do not have an agenda (that is, they are not policy makers or health and social care practitioners, for example), and when the intention of participatory research is simply to raise public consciousness, then it may be enough simply to 'view and enjoy' pictorial evidence.

However, while we would not wish to use the photographic evidence in this study to depict or confer meaning in ways that would misrepresent or misinterpret the experiences of the participants involved, it is important to recognise the need for integrative approaches in respect of the publication of findings that facilitate both faithful presentation and analysis of findings (by researchers, for example) in order to inform diverse audiences who may have different agendas.

If people with learning difficulties are unable, or less able, to challenge dominant systems, then it is equally clear that they also have limited opportunities to develop their own ways of highlighting their health and social care needs. In this respect, it becomes the responsibility of others to represent their interests in broader, political contexts.

Photographs taken by participants with learning difficulties

Conclusion

This research study was intended both to raise awareness in respect of the benefits of STH for vulnerable groups and to help inform health and social care policy and practice in terms of the social inclusion needs of these groups. Using different research methods for different groups, depending on the nature of their vulnerability, enables us to achieve both these objectives. Thus, photographic participation and elicitation methods, as part of a multi-method approach, fit well in the broader context of this study.

As a research method *on its own*, photographic elicitation may be limited in respect of providing evidence (particularly of the kind that may have social and political consequences) to wider audiences, but used in a flexible or integrative way and as part of a multi-dimensional approach, photographic elicitation may provide important and valuable 'evidence' that other methods may miss. As Donaldson (2001) has argued, "photographs should not be compared to some hypothetical absolute truth, but only to other data collection methods. In that company, they look pretty good" (p 6).

Garden projects and environmental philosophies

Recently, *Growth Point*, the magazine of the charity Thrive, devoted one of its issues to a series of articles about sustainable development and organic growing in relation to STH (see *Growth Point*, 2004, issue 97). Many issues were explored in the articles and sustainable initiatives at garden projects were described. It is clear, both from these articles and from contact with practitioners, that there is an interest in sustainable development and an engagement by garden projects with the environmental and biodiversity agendas. For example, 240 projects (29%) of the 836 that responded to the national survey in our study reported that they had a wildlife garden and 44 projects in the survey had a sustainable form of energy supply – either wind or solar power (or both in some cases). A small number of projects (15) also reported that their project area was a conservation site or woodland. However, from visits to project sites it can be seen that many other projects are also actively involved in conservation work on a smaller scale as part of their activities. Of the projects visited in this research, four were involved in conservation work and two of those had produced detailed plans for major conservation projects. Organic gardening techniques were also a feature of many STH projects. Seventeen of the projects visited used such methods and one was registered with the Soil Association as organic. The process involved in such registration is a lengthy one and therefore shows the commitment of that particular project to this form of horticulture.

Additionally, two of the projects practiced 'biodynamic gardening', an extension of organic gardening in which planting and horticultural activities are carried out according to the lunar calendar. Other environmentally sustainable activities included recycling and composting schemes. Environmental issues are therefore an integral part of the philosophy and aims of many garden projects and so require closer analysis.

Some garden projects advertise and promote their organic approach in their literature or their choice of project name. This not only signals their interest in the field, it also serves to recruit volunteers (and sometimes clients) with similar lifestyle preferences and ideological commitments. Many of the volunteers that were interviewed were initially attracted to their project by the environmental dimension, for example:

> "Well, what I think what brought me into it initially was the fact that they were doing small-scale demonstration projects to indicate a different way of living – the sustainable development projects. So, it was the environmental aspects of it that brought me in. You know, like the little wind turbine and composting toilets and organic gardening.

> "... and I was so impressed with what could be done on such a small site, you know, a fairly small site in the middle of [town]." (Lyn, volunteer, project for people with learning difficulties)

The organic 'tag', therefore, may act as a banner to rally like-minded individuals and bring them together with others, interested not only in organic gardening, but in the wider issues of sustainability, including also the care of vulnerable people in society. This common ideology secures a bond between project members, particularly staff and volunteers, and may also include clients, many of whom appeared interested in issues of sustainability and had been attracted to specific projects because of their organic gardening activities. The underlying philosophy that links projects' organic activities with those wider environmental and social issues appeared to have been well developed and carefully constructed by some project managers who were keen to spread that message:

> "It [organic gardening] meets a whole lot of environmental concerns that people have got and in our society. People are very much disempowered in those specific terms....

> "... so we're taking people who are dependent consumers on markets and giving them some small component of independence from that large system and in terms of personal empowerment, that is a very powerful mechanism for realising that they're not completely at the bottom of the pile and they have got some autonomy and self-decision in their lives and that would be really important, and also with the value of food being very highly valued in financial terms in the current society, we

re-value the food that we grow because we're putting our time and energy into it and that gives us a very different reading of value, so rather than valuing food in purely monetary terms we're valuing it in terms of personal and social coherence really and that would be one quick way of summing up, that this food growing, horticulture side of things is very much a thermometer of the social coherence of, whether it's a community or a society, but if it's still got that component then that is still valued, that is a foundation of its self confidence as a society or as a group community or individuals." (Matthew, project organiser, organic garden project)

The practice of organic gardening at projects should, therefore, not be viewed simply in the context of producing good quality, wholesome food, but in the wider social context of the environmental agenda and this, itself, may be beneficial. The manager of a project for people with mental health problems suggested that clients perceived organic gardening to be "a good thing" and that they "fundamentally feel that they are part of a good thing, that preserving the environment is a good thing". Thus they identify with the goals of sustainability and recognise "that nature matters", and that preserving nature is a "good thing". Such an attitude, he suggested, influenced his clients' well-being and recovery. Therefore, by participating in a project that is involved in environmentally sustainable practices, clients may feel that they are doing something about the environmental needs of the planet:

"I think it makes you feel good about it because it's, like, fresher vegetables and the produce tastes better.

"Yeah! Yeah, and it's good for the environment, as well.

"I care about it because otherwise you end up with, end up with none of the earth left, otherwise, if we didn't have stuff, gardens like this." (Shirley, project client, with mental ill health)

Some of the clients, particularly those with learning difficulties, were not able to understand fully the environmental ethos of the project but were encouraged to participate in it. Such actions may broaden the experiences of clients and may form part of the process of education and training at the projects:

"... they might not understand that but now, thinking of one person in particular, if she sees anyone put a tin can in the bin, she'll tell them, 'No, you can recycle that', and a lot of people start to bring their cans and newspapers from home, and they quite enjoy doing that as well. So I think they do start to understand a bit of the concept of recycling." (Jill, project worker, speaking about clients with learning difficulties)

Issues of health do play a part in the clients' (and staff's) perception and value of organic food and participation in project activities. The health aspect of the outdoor environment is discussed on page 45 and perceptions of health and well-being are examined on page 82 and only those issues related to organic gardening and sustainability are addressed here. Many of the participants of projects were able to take home produce that they and their colleagues have grown, although no food was grown at some of the projects visited and at others the quantities available to clients were limited. In all, 17 of the projects visited were involved in food cultivation and all of those used organic methods without the use of chemical herbicides or pesticides. The projects actively encouraged their clients to take food home and provided guidance on cooking and food preparation so that clients who lived in residential accommodation with limited access to a kitchen were able to benefit. Where food was grown, 91% of clients took produce home, and almost a third (32.3%) reported that they bought more fresh fruit and vegetables as a result of their experience of cultivation. Organic food was seen as 'healthy' and in sharp contrast to that available in supermarkets, which was regarded with mistrust. One client called such produce "lies" and even regarded supermarket food labelled as 'organic' with suspicion, as its provenance was unknown:

> "... you've seen the whole process, you know what's gone into it, you know that there's been no chemical near there, you know there's no lies, you've done it yourself, there's no additives, preservatives, there's no, nothing of that, there's no lies, it's pure, clean.

> "You know, everything that goes into it, and this is what I'm finding in the supermarkets, there's lies, they say things are organic and, unfortunately, I personally believe that perhaps it's not up to the standard of [the project]." (Brian, client/volunteer, organic garden project)

Some project staff (and one client) drew parallels between the use of chemicals in the environment and the ingestion of chemicals and other toxic substances. The planet was a metaphor for the human body that was being poisoned by chemicals, drugs and even medication. Sustainable environmental practices, therefore, would lead to less pollution of the planet and such practices would lead to the health of the individual:

> "I mean, it's not something that we promote but it's a reality, of course, that they've abused their bodies through substances that are poisonous. And so, to grow organically is, you know, is a complement to what we're actually trying to do with the physical well-being of each individual. So, filling oneself with food that's, that hasn't got substances or chemicals attached to them is, you know, it all, sort of, complements each other, really." (Ann, organiser, project for people recovering from substance misuse)

In general the organic approach to food cultivation was seen as part of a holistic approach to health and analogies were made between the principles of organic gardening and the process of achieving health. Projects were seen as a means to providing health not only through the organic, unpolluted food but also by the associated activities and lifestyle and by searching out optimum conditions for health in a similar way to which conditions are selected for organic cultivation. Organic methods also required the use of physical labour, rather than that of machines or chemicals. This promoted physical exercise and health. The use of increased physical labour was also considered to improve social interaction.

"I think it's towards the organic philosophy, really. A philosophy of health rather than a philosophy of treating illness, because in organic gardening you don't treat symptoms.

"You look for friends, you look for allies in the insect world, and you look for optimum health conditions. So, if you can encourage people to do the same in their own health. So, that's looking for allies, looking for friends, looking for people that help them stay well, and also looking for the best conditions, which is usually around sleep, hygiene, exercise, and diet." (Sally, volunteer, project for people with learning difficulties)

Producing food to eat may also raise the self-esteem of the clients as their efforts at cultivation produce food that is *intrinsically* valuable, that is, it is nourishing in its own right. While money is valuable it has to be used to buy food. It cannot, itself, be consumed. Hence the production of food was held in high regard and many references were made to 'self-sufficiency' and the satisfaction of growing food to eat. Although clients were not truly self-sufficient and probably relied on commercial sources for the bulk of their food, they were able to produce some food by their own efforts, without recourse to chemicals or other 'artificial' means, and so were able to bypass retailers and supermarkets for some of the time. The ability to grow food also differentiated clients from those people (the general public) who did not grow food or did not have the skills and knowledge to do it. This, too, appeared to elevate self-esteem. Project workers encouraged the link with 'traditional' food production and biodynamic gardening, practiced at two projects, was seen by one project organiser as "a folk tradition of gardening – a route back to the base concepts of food production".

Biodynamic gardening (see Thun, 1999; Wright, 2003) contends that cosmic forces, particularly the lunar cycle and the astronomical position of the moon relative to the constellations of the Zodiac, affect plant growth and development. Therefore, the planting of seeds and other horticultural activities are carried out according to a lunar planting calendar. The principles, however, are not based on a belief in supernatural influences but on supposed natural forces unrecognised by modern science. The adoption of such methods may add to the perceived value of food produced in this way because of the specialist knowledge possessed by the gardeners, which is not held (or is deliberately ignored) by those practising mainstream horticulture or agriculture.

Conclusion

Clients' involvement in organic gardening methods is perceived to produce benefits not only through the improvement of their dietary habits by access to high-quality produce (although this may be limited), but also through their engagement with an environmental ideology that is generally regarded as benign. Clients' well-being may be improved because they perceive themselves to be involved in activities that are not harmful or destructive and which may be beneficial to the environment.

The organic philosophy is well developed in the minds of project managers and workers and there is often a desire to disseminate that philosophy, for example, to encourage project volunteers to start new organic projects, and also by the teaching of organic methods either as part of the daily process of horticulture at the gardens or by setting more formal training programmes.

5 Discussion

Promoting social inclusion

People with poor mental or physical health are often at greatest risk of social exclusion (Social Exclusion Unit, 2004: www.socialexclusionunit.gov.uk).

Too often, vulnerable people are excluded from society, marginalised and overlooked and must live their lives as individuals rather than as members of society with important contributions to make. For individuals, and particularly for individuals with poor physical or mental health, a critical factor in feeling 'included' in society and contributing to its maintenance is in feeling socially and politically included. Burchardt and colleagues (2002) make reference to these dimensions in their work on social exclusion, and we have used these, and other dimensions, in this investigation of the benefits of STH for vulnerable groups.

We know, and have emphasised throughout this report, that people with serious health and other problems are often excluded from society because of their conditions and personal circumstances and that they are often subject to, at best, misunderstanding and misconception and, at worst, prejudice, discrimination and harassment (see also Aldridge and Becker, 2003). We also know that it is important that determined efforts are made to challenge the social exclusion of vulnerable groups and one of the ways in which this can occur is through the use of social therapies and practices to help people with distinct health and social care needs. Social and therapeutic horticulture can play a key role here, as the research evidence in this report has shown.

Informing policy and practice through research

Research is important in providing an evidence base that can help to inform and shape health and social care policy and practice. Previously, as we showed in our review of STH literature (see Sempik et al, 2003), this evidence was limited and, in many cases, research lacked methodological rigour. While it is difficult to demonstrate directly the influence of research on policy and practice, the value of evidence in this respect is not questioned (see Becker and Bryman, 2004). In respect of STH it was clear that more research was needed in order to highlight its therapeutic significance for vulnerable groups.

Our research investigation undoubtedly helps to breach this evidential gap. The combination of different and inclusive methodological approaches, the volume and richness of data collated, and the use of personal accounts from participants themselves all contribute to the value of the evidence collated and its usefulness in respect of informing health and social care policy and practice in the UK.

While there is a scientific tradition of using quantitative methods when investigating human experience, including, for example, health and well-being measures and randomised controlled trials, inclusive or participative approaches are gaining increasing recognition and credibility in both social and medical sciences, particularly when used among vulnerable groups. The aim of our study was to examine the experiences of these groups in respect of STH; to do so without the use of humanistic and inclusive methods would have compromised both the subjects of the research themselves and the outcomes. Walmsley and Johnson (2003) have argued that research needs to be both 'academically rigorous' as well as useful "to the people who are subject to it, which is relevant to their needs and can inform and promote social change" (p 9).

The evidence we present in this report shows the wide number of ways in which clients of STH projects benefit from attendance at projects and more broadly in their daily lives. Positive outcomes here are undeniable and range from the highly personal to the social and political. Clients of STH projects use them for their own personal gain (relaxation, reflection, restoration), in order to build self-esteem and confidence as well as to further their education and skills and to extend social networks. However, one of the critical questions to ask in a broader sense, is 'why horticulture and gardening?' as well as considering whether other, alternative or complementary therapies or activities could not be equally beneficial to vulnerable adults.

The answer to these questions is, of course, far from straightforward. There is no reason, for example, why a range of different social therapies or practices should not be used in promoting social inclusion for vulnerable people. However, trying to confer value and credibility on some of these practices from the point of view of formal health and social care policy and practice would perhaps be less of an easy task, and particularly where there is a dearth of research evidence in these areas.

However, our evidence suggests that STH has a number of contributions to make in respect of promoting social inclusion for vulnerable adults and that outcomes here compare more than favourably to the various dimensions of social inclusion recognised more broadly in the social sciences (see Burchardt et al, 2002). Furthermore, some of the benefits of STH may also be located in other therapies and practices but, as we have shown throughout this report, are certainly specific to the breadth and richness of gardening and horticultural practice. With reference to the dimensions of social inclusion, STH outcomes can be described in the following ways:

- *diverse and multi-dimensional activity:* planting, cultivating, growing, nurturing as well as physical work, such as digging, constructing and so on;
- *contributing to production:* through work, education, training and marketing and selling produce;
- *consumption:* planting, growing and consuming food that contributes to the quality of life of clients;

- *increased social opportunities:* horticulture offers a way for people who attend gardening projects, and others in the wider community who share an interest in horticulture, to engage in reciprocal relationships. The socially therapeutic aspects of these projects work by generating and sustaining an interest in gardening that is shared by all (irrespective of ability); by overcoming prejudice and stereotype through increased contact between vulnerable (socially excluded) and non-vulnerable (socially included) members of society; and by an acceptance of vulnerable adults – through regular gardening activity – who make a valuable contribution to the wider community. For project staff there are a number of other objectives, not least to physically maintain the garden and sustain the project itself. It is a happy synchronicity that sees clients contributing to these and other objectives by working alongside other clients and project workers, who often also become their friends;
- *the politics of the personal:* STH projects offer clients opportunities for self-reflection, relaxation and restoration as well as building self-confidence and challenging the perceptions (and misconceptions) of others by providing clients with the opportunity and environment in which to demonstrate their *abilities* (as opposed to disabilities).

Mechanisms and processes

A model of STH revisited

In our review of the literature (Sempik et al, 2003) we presented a model of the processes involved in providing health and well-being as a result of either participating in horticultural activities or experiencing the natural environment in which such activities could take place. This model was based on the published literature and is reproduced in Figure 5.1.

At the base of the model lay the mechanisms that determined the inherent appeal of the natural environment. This provided the context for both the passive appreciation of landscape (and the garden environment) and the active participation in horticulture and gardening. Active gardening was associated with a number of outcomes, such as the development of skills, social processes and possible employment. This in turn led to acceptance, inclusion and rehabilitation. Passive appreciation of nature was associated with tranquillity, peace and spirituality. However, all of these steps were interconnected and pointed to health and well-being at the summit of the model (see Sempik et al, 2003, pp 47-8). While findings from this study broadly support such a model they can be used to refine it.

The environmental and natural dimensions were specified only as 'innate factors – evolutionary – biophilia'. These appeared in many forms throughout the literature and were taken to provide the backdrop that facilitated the restorative experience in the context of attention restoration theory and recovery from stress. Results from this study have shown that

Figure 5.1: A simple model of some of the processes, activities and outcomes of STH as described in the literature

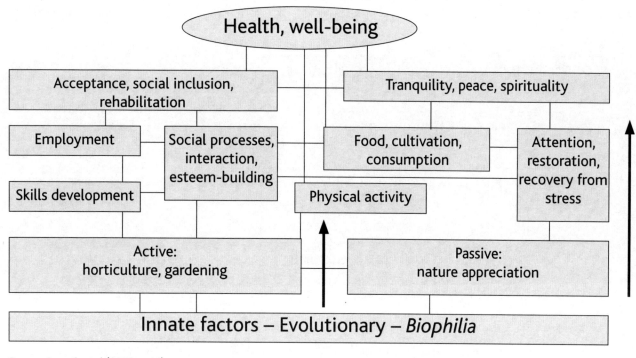

Source: Sempik et al (2003, p 46)

the natural component of the model is multifaceted – project participants gave a number of reasons for their enjoyment and appreciation of the natural environment associated with the theme of 'being outside'. These included an escape from an inferior environment (related to the *being away* component of the restorative environment), the association of open air with health, a sense of place with regard to the garden project site, fascination with nature itself and a desire to engage with natural processes by nurturing plants and a connectedness with nature or spiritual bond. These dimensions are summarised in Figure 5.2 and form the base layer of the new model, which is shown in Figure 5.3. The natural environment not only acts as a backdrop for the activities and processes shown, but may also have an effect in its own right. Experience of the environment,

Figure 5.2: The 'natural' dimension of STH

Open air and health – escape
Contact with nature – fascination
Engagement with the natural process – nuture
Connectedness with nature – spiritual
Lack of pressure – peacefulness
Sense of place

Figure 5.3: A summary of activities, processes and outcomes associated with STH as observed in research findings

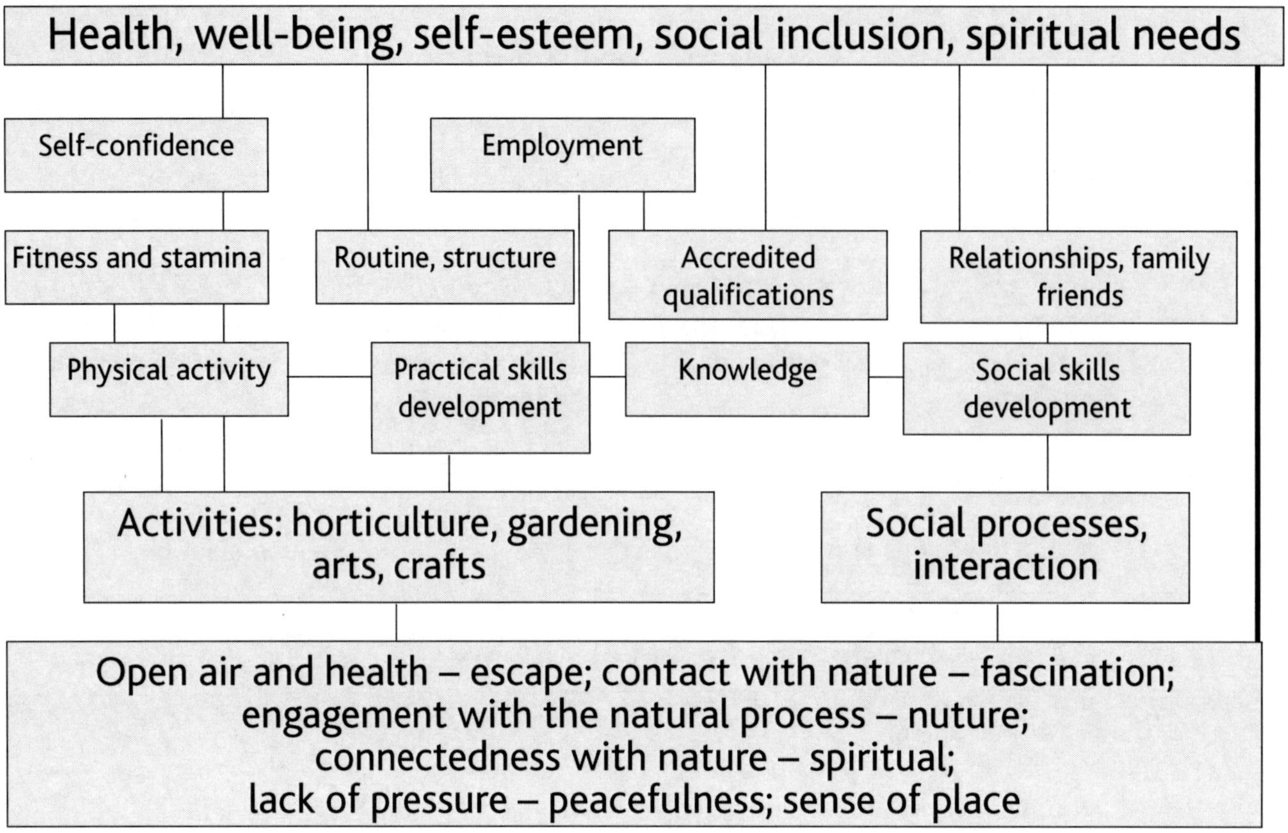

Health, well-being, self-esteem, social inclusion, spiritual needs

Self-confidence		Employment		
Fitness and stamina	Routine, structure		Accredited qualifications	Relationships, family friends
Physical activity	Practical skills development	Knowledge		Social skills development

Activities: horticulture, gardening, arts, crafts

Social processes, interaction

Open air and health – escape; contact with nature – fascination; engagement with the natural process – nuture; connectedness with nature – spiritual; lack of pressure – peacefulness; sense of place

and interaction with it, may promote well-being through the restoration of attention; it may also satisfy a spiritual dimension related to a sense of purpose, meaning and a connection to nature.

The other outcomes and processes are similar to those of the original model but there has been a slight change in emphasis and arrangement of the components. For example, the dimensions of 'routine' and 'relationships' have been added to the new model, and that of 'spirituality' has been subsumed into both the lowest and highest levels of the original model. As mentioned above, it appears that this element may be experienced both by engagement with a natural environment, thereby experiencing a connection to nature, and by participation in activities that provide meaning and purpose.

The model summarises, and generalises, the findings of this research with regard to the activities and processes observed at garden projects. Other dimensions may be added that are specific to particular projects or environments. The outcomes are shown as 'Health, well-being, self-esteem, social inclusion and spiritual needs'; we believe that the research evidence presented here shows that projects practising STH do indeed provide such benefits.

Indications and limitations

Indications

As this research shows, horticulture and garden projects are used for a wide range of vulnerable groups, including people with mental health problems, learning difficulties, physical disabilities, older people and others. This suggests that there may be no specific indications for referring clients to such projects other than the risk of exclusion (due to, or associated with, a lack of meaningful activity and social opportunities) often associated with the increased risk of physical illness or diseases caused by the lack of opportunity for physical activity or active leisure. However, there does appear to be an active selection process within the system of referral although this may frequently operate on an ad hoc basis. The occupational therapists and mental health nurses who were interviewed in the course of the research did not refer many clients to projects but appeared to be careful in their choice of candidate. Eight of these practitioners had been referring clients for between one and five years and had referred an average of around eight clients each (by their estimates) in that time. The decision to refer clients was based on a subjective assessment of each case, taking into account, for example, a client's expressed interest in gardening or being outside. Disruptive or difficult clients were generally not referred to projects although some project organisers appeared to be able to provide a one-to-one service for clients with the greatest support needs and were prepared to take on difficult clients. A number of occupational therapists responded that they had difficulty in deciding who to refer and would have found some formal guidelines to be useful (see page 128). When asked about the specific condition or illness of patients who responded favourably to attending horticulture projects three of the health practitioners mentioned schizophrenia and depressive illnesses:

> "I think there are people, the illnesses tend to be schizophrenia, and depressive illnesses. And the other group that I've found it helpful for is people who's lives, erm, have been blighted, if you like, in adult life by childhood sexual abuse." (community mental health nurse)

> "Mainly that the clients that suffer from schizophrenia.

> "I think it's because there isn't much out in the community. There's only, like, day hospitals, and, that they want to get out and do something and be with public and try and get back to a normal life. And, and, talk to normal people, as they would say. It's the interaction with the community as well.

> "And sometimes as well, it's the fact that, quite a lot of it is lone working as well and they don't like to be bothered with other people." (mental health nurse)

They suggested that the particular type of project activities enabled the clients to mix with others if they wished, but also gave them personal space if they wanted to be alone. There also appeared to be few alternative activities.

No information was available as to how many patients or clients immediately rejected the whole notion of gardening, or how many prospective clients declined to participate in the project after an initial visit, or the number who stayed for a very short time at a project and then decided that the activities were not suitable or enjoyable for them.

There was no coercion for clients to join a project, or to stay at one and no financial incentive or imperative. Over a period of a year the turnover of clients was low, a small number found employment or training posts and left projects, and a small number left with no obvious place in mind, but the majority of clients were still there after 12 months. The client group, therefore, is one for whom gardening and the related activities described earlier are compatible, or at the very least, acceptable. With this in mind it is not surprising that the respondents in this research spoke favourably of their experiences of attending projects. It would appear that occupational therapists and other health practitioners have been successful in identifying and referring responsive clients to garden projects. Clients need to be responsive in order to benefit, because the process is not a passive one such as medication, but an active one in which the clients need to engage. Indeed, the notion of *compatibility* is one of the key dimensions of the 'restorative environment' in Attention Restoration Theory (see Kaplan and Kaplan, 1989, pp 177-200). What is unclear, however, is how universal such acceptance of STH projects would be among a wider group of people with mental health problems, learning difficulties and other vulnerabilities. Would many more people participate in such projects if they were given the opportunity?

Limitations

There appear to be no reports in the literature concerning negative aspects of STH or contraindications for it. While it may not be suitable for everyone, or appeal to everyone, there are no accounts of any specific ill effects associated with it. Accidents and injury do occur in the home and garden and therefore it would not be unreasonable to assume that they also occur at garden projects; however, none of the people interviewed in the course of the research expressed any undue concern about the dangers of gardening. Project workers were keen to indicate that due care and supervision were exercised and that proper training was provided. Various forms of risk assessment were also carried out (issues of risk assessment are discussed in *Growing together* – see Sempik et al, 2005). Physical disability, cognitive impairment, challenging behaviour and mental ill health were not seen as barriers to participation in garden projects and projects were often able to provide one-to-one supervision for clients with major needs. Care workers accompanied some of the clients in order to provide such a service, for example, one client with learning difficulties was prone to wandering off and needed constant supervision to prevent him doing so. His support worker (like others who we observed) engaged in the gardening activities (digging, weeding and planting) alongside the client. However, all of the projects operated with limited resources and finances and the extent to which they could offer intensive supervision was also limited. One of the barriers to participation by those with major support needs is likely to be the limitation in resources of the projects. Projects must balance the needs of clients with the availability of resources; it is possible that some clients may have difficulty accessing projects because of their high support needs. Such clients may be screened out by referring agencies and professionals or quite simply refused by project organisers who only have the capacity to deal with small numbers of clients with such needs. Further research is needed to examine the availability of garden projects to those with the greatest support needs.

Health professionals and project organisers reported that they had encountered few negative effects of projects. Some aspects of projects did not suit particular individuals, for example, a small number of clients did not enjoy cultivating a communal plot but wanted exclusive rights or ownership of part of the garden. Small individual plots were provided by some of the projects and cultivation of these gave clients a sense of possession and stake in 'their own' part of land. Some clients lost interest in projects and drifted away, some had been disruptive or difficult and had to be removed while others who had been difficult at day centres were found to be accommodating at garden projects. As already mentioned, the turnover of clients at projects was low.

A few difficulties had been encountered as a result of relationships between clients, for example, one client with an alcohol problem had found a drinking partner at a project and this had compounded his difficulties.

One project organiser reported on the case of a client who had become difficult and abusive at home after attending a project (see page 56) and suggested that he had gained "too much confidence", which had led him to behave like a "superhero". Such reactions are probably rare and this was the only case encountered in the course of the study.

Some project organisers were concerned that clients could become too dependent on a project and so would not be able to move on and progress (into employment or training) as a result. While this could be an issue at projects that are specifically aimed at finding employment for their clients, it is less likely to be important at other projects that accept that the clients' stay is likely to be long and that progress may be slow. Such progress is also likely to occur more frequently within the context of the project rather than by a move away from it (as this research has shown).

All of the clients reported that they enjoyed attending the project in some measure; however, some expressed the view that they would have liked 'proper' employment and the financial reward that this would bring, as the following statement shows:

> **"But I still have times when I think I'm affected by not working full-time in paid work only.**
>
> **"There's something about receiving the money in your hand that's, kind of, a statement of self-worth somehow." (Ken, client, nursery garden project for clients with mental ill health)**

While projects provide most clients with a sense of status and self-esteem, derived from their role and activities, any financial reward is limited (see page 76). To some clients even this income is welcome and adds to self-esteem, while to others it may highlight their perceived inadequacy in the labour market. Until recently the benefits of *employment* have been contrasted with the health and well-being problems caused by *unemployment*. However, recent research is beginning to focus on *underemployment*, which can be defined "in terms of the adequacy of the exchange within the labour market between the household (usually operationalized ... by such measures as individual worker's hours and income) and the economy, and fairness is the criterion used to determine the adequacy of the exchange" (see Friedland and Price, 2003, p 34). Underemployment is, therefore, part of a continuum between full employment and unemployment. In this context underemployment can be in terms of skill utilisation, hours worked or income. While garden projects successfully address the first two issues (and provide other benefits normally associated with employment), few can provide a proper wage by the standards of the marketplace. This lack of financial reward could adversely affect some clients. Indeed, there is evidence to suggest that underemployed workers report poorer health and well-being than fully employed workers (see Dooley, 2003; Friedland and Price, 2003). However, the relative importance of the utilisation of skills, hours spent at work and income have not been satisfactorily investigated for those in employment and further research is necessary to investigate whether lack of income is an important issue to clients attending STH projects, that is, whether they perceive themselves to be underemployed. Clients appeared to value the lack of pressure associated with project 'work' and recognised that paid work brought pressure and they may therefore be willing to trade financial reward for other benefits.

Conclusion

At present, referral to garden projects by health and social care professionals has been on a case-by-case basis. The opportunities for meaningful activities and social interaction are likely to benefit many different clients who find themselves isolated by illness, impairment or social circumstances. The formulation of formal guidelines for referral may useful (see page 128) but such guidelines should not be used to exclude potential clients but to identify those who have not been offered a place at a project and who may find it beneficial. Further research is necessary to investigate whether the lack of financial reward is an important issue for some clients attending STH projects.

Implications for policy and practice

Recognition of garden projects as useful promoters of health and social care

These research findings show that STH is a useful and effective aspect of health and social care provision. Garden projects often provide a welcome alternative to day centres and although they may not be appropriate for all people requiring some form of day care, this research shows that projects provide benefits of health and well-being to many different vulnerable groups and individuals. The costs, per client session, of attending STH projects are similar to those of NHS day care but in many cases projects charge lower fees because of receipt of funding from other sources, including grants and commercial activities. While charging low fees may, in some cases, act to the detriment of projects it may also make the use of them attractive to those commissioning care services. An increased awareness of the existence of STH projects and their activities, by health and social care professionals and those responsible for procuring services, may lead to an increased uptake of such services.

Benefiting and enabling a contribution to society through different concepts of 'work'

We have discussed how STH project activities provide clients with the opportunity to engage in *production* as seen in the terms of the framework of social inclusion. However, the concept of 'production' and 'work' are still firmly linked to paid employment in the eyes of many. It is important, therefore, that the contribution to society of project *work*, and other such activities, is recognised and valued accordingly:

"We all want to make it possible for everyone to contribute to society through 'work'. This way of seeing, caring for everyone and involving everyone, is now enshrined within the principles of sustainable development and sustainable communities. This piece of research has given us an insight into what 'work' means for various vulnerable groups of society. Set within a structured environment, with support, training and encouragement, they are seen to be able to make a real contribution to society and benefit from a feeling of personal worth. I propose that accepting different concepts of work would enable society to get into a win-win situation. It means going on to purposefully create situations in which different people are supported to contribute according to their ability to do so, and in doing so, protect vulnerable members of society." (Judy Ling Wong OBE, Director, Black Environment Network)

Awareness of STH projects and the attitudes of health professionals

Horticulture and related activities have been used in occupational therapy for many years; however, it is not known how many therapists presently use horticulture as an activity in therapy and how many also refer clients to garden projects. Further research should be carried out to investigate the extent of the use of horticulture in this context and the level of awareness of local services and national support from organisations such as Thrive. While all of the health and social care professionals interviewed for this study were positive about the use of horticulture, either as an activity for occupational therapy or in the form of organised gardening projects, some suggested that senior health practitioners may be sceptical about STH as a useful activity. Further work should be carried out to explore the attitudes of this group and also to publish findings about the activities, processes and outcomes for clients who participate in such projects.

Information, specifically targeted at general practitioners (GPs), describing the benefits of STH and details of local projects, should be prepared and distributed to them through Primary Care Trusts. Information for the general public can also be distributed through GPs' surgeries and by agencies such as the regional Public Health Observatories. Potential clients will then be able to ask for referral for themselves, or those with caring responsibilities may ask for a referral for those for whom they care.

Guidelines for referral to projects

The findings of this research suggest that occupational therapists are careful in their choice of client for referral. Presently no guidelines are available to help practitioners, such as occupational therapists and Community Mental Health Teams, decide who to refer to projects and much referral is done on an ad hoc basis taking into account, for example, past interest in gardening, the wishes of a client to work outside and the availability of places. Preparation of a set of guidelines for referral of clients to STH projects could help many health and social care practitioners, especially those who are not familiar with such projects or are new to the profession (see also previous section on awareness raising and the information outputs, page 128). This would require the cooperation of health professionals (occupational therapists, community psychiatric nurses, psychiatrists, social workers) who have experience with patients and also STH project staff. It would also need an organisation or agency, such as the College of Occupational Therapists or Thrive, to oversee and coordinate this work.

Expansion of STH projects to other vulnerable groups

At present the majority of users of STH projects are those with mental health problems and learning difficulties. This (and other) research shows that while many other groups of users do participate in STH projects, their numbers are fewer. Ways should be explored, therefore, of enabling other vulnerable groups to access STH projects where possible and appropriate. This may also be related to awareness raising an information output.

An examination of the type of services offered by projects to different groups should be carried out. There is evidence from this research that there may be differences in the level of service offered to different client groups. For example, the data suggest that people with learning difficulties are more likely to be offered the opportunity for accredited training than people with mental health problems. Is this because of a lower demand for such training among people with mental health problems? Should anything be done to increase the level of accredited training and would people with mental health problems benefit from such an increase? These and similar questions can be asked of project organisers and the practitioners who refer clients to those projects.

Under-representation of women and black and minority ethnic groups at STH projects

The apparent under-representation of women and black and minority ethnic groups at STH projects should be investigated. There may be parallels between black and minority ethnic participation in STH and in their participation in the natural environment, for example, visits to the national parks and the countryside. Cooperation with organisations such as the Black Environment Network and the Women's Environmental Network may help to identify the issues involved and these may influence the preparation and distribution of material for raising awareness of STH and projects.

Involvement of projects in the research process

Project staff can be encouraged to participate in the collection and analysis of data on the outcomes for clients at STH projects; this could include information on client turnover, numbers finding employment or training posts in addition to 'soft outcomes' such as measures of progress. This would require a central collection or pooling of data and the involvement of an organisation or agency to coordinate the work. However, such an enterprise would produce a steady stream of data on the benefits and outcomes for clients.

The use and value of qualitative data

Presently, Randomised Controlled Trials (RCTs) are regarded as the 'gold standard' of research methods by those involved in biomedical research and those who draft policy in that field. The value of qualitative research methods is often overlooked and sometimes derided. However, activities such as STH frequently do not lend themselves to the type of quantitative methodology typified by RCTs. Indeed, the process of randomisation can be unethical in some cases. There is a need, therefore, for researchers to raise awareness among policy makers (and other researchers in the medical and health arena) of the value of qualitative research methods. The acceptance that qualitative methods, such as interviews and narratives, can provide useful biomedical data is already becoming more widely acknowledged, for example, the work of Radley and Taylor (2003), who used photographic elicitation techniques to study patients' experience of recovery in hospital, has been discussed on page 15.

While RCTs may not be suitable for all research into STH, it is possible that certain aspects or activities may be suited to such methods. What is required is a detailed study of the feasibility of using RCT in this context. This should encompass not only the question of the random allocation of participants to the various groups within the study but also the development of instruments (questionnaires and other tools) that are specific and sensitive enough to detect changes in health and well-being, which are likely to be subtle. The development of such instruments will not only enable the successful completion of an RCT (if it is indeed appropriate) but their widespread application will also provide information with which to compare other activities and therapies.

The role of garden projects for physical health promotion for vulnerable people

There is considerable evidence to suggest that the physical health of people with learning difficulties and mental ill health is poorer than that of the general population (this has been discussed on page 82). There is evidence to show that levels of obesity are higher in these groups (see Bell and Bhate, 1992; Daumit et al, 2003) and that psychiatric medication predisposes patients to weight gain and obesity (see Schwartz et al, 2004). Additionally, the lifestyles of some people with mental health problems have been shown to be 'unhealthy' (Brown et al, 1999), with a high usage of cigarettes and alcohol, poor diet and inadequate exercise. While these vulnerable groups may be exposed to more risk factors for physical ill health than the general population, they also appear to be excluded from many of the sport and leisure activities that could help to protect them from those risks. Garden projects (and also Green Gyms) offer an opportunity, specifically for these and other excluded groups, to engage in physical activity that may lead to improved fitness and health. The role of projects in providing such activities, therefore, needs to be recognised and extended by inclusion in health strategies for people with mental ill health, learning and other difficulties. Some STH projects already provide health advice, for example, on issues such as obesity, physical activity and smoking. There is still, however, an opportunity for them to become more involved in health promotion and for those who formulate health strategies to use projects to distribute information and also to help enact some of the policies.

A professional status for practitioners of STH?

Practitioners of STH in the UK have a wide variety of qualifications and experience, both in the area of health and social care and also in horticulture and gardening. Qualifications include those in occupational therapy, nursing, teaching and social care. Additionally, around 40% of projects had staff who were trained in various forms of horticulture and had qualifications including degrees, HNCs, HNDs and NVQs. Ten per cent of projects had staff with qualifications in therapeutic horticulture (including the professional development certificate or diploma offered by Coventry University). The diverse knowledge and skills of staff probably adds to the richness of the resources and experiences (both for clients and staff) at garden projects. However, it is possible that the lack of a single qualification or professional registration may lead to a diminution in the perceived value of STH projects by senior health practitioners and policy makers. In the US, the American Horticultural Therapy Association provides a voluntary registration scheme, based on qualifications and experience, for practitioners in addition to disseminating information about research and training and raising awareness about the use of horticulture as a 'therapeutic' process. One of its stated aims is to "establish professional standards and a credentialing process for horticultural therapy practitioners" (see www.ahta.org: 'About AHTA'). It is likely that such registration leads to an enhanced professional status of both practitioners and practice (and possibly also improved remuneration). No such process operates in the UK although a voluntary quality assurance and accreditation scheme for projects has been developed and is due to be launched by Thrive in 2005. Voluntary self-regulation of other complementary therapies (including professional registration) has taken place and is encouraged by the government and such a process may also be useful for STH practitioners. Research should be undertaken, therefore, to identify whether registration of STH practitioners is necessary or desirable in the UK and whether the lack of a registration process will be a barrier to receiving funds and client referrals from the NHS and social services departments in the future. Also, if registration or regulation are deemed desirable, what form or structure should a professional association take and how should it be organised? Organisations involved with practitioners of STH, including the College of Occupational Therapists, Thrive, Coventry University and others should cooperate in undertaking such research and the implementation of its findings.

References

Aldridge, J. and Becker, S. (2003) *Children caring for parents with mental illness: Perspectives of young carers, parents and professionals*, Bristol: The Policy Press.

Arksey, H. (1996) 'Collecting data through joint interviews', *Social Research Update*, issue 15, Guildford: Department of Sociology, University of Surrey.

Arksey, H. (2004) 'Semi-structured and unstructured interviewing', in S. Becker and A. Bryman (eds) *Understanding research methods for social policy and practice*, Bristol: The Policy Press, pp 268-75.

Becker, S. (2004) 'What research action should we use to judge whether a therapeutic intervention is effective?', in S. Becker (ed) *Improving behaviour through therapeutic approaches*, Nottingham: Excellence in Cities, pp 51-3.

Becker, S. and Bryman, A. (2004) 'Evidence and knowledge', in S. Becker and A. Bryman (eds) *Understanding research methods for social policy and practice*, Bristol: The Policy Press, pp 40-59.

Bell, A. and Bhate, M. (1992) 'Prevalence of overweight and obesity in Down's Syndrome and other mentally handicapped adults living in the community', *Journal of Intellectual Disability Research*, vol 36, pp 359-64.

Bhatti, M. and Church, A. (2000) '"I never promised you a rose garden": gender, leisure and home-making', *Leisure Studies*, vol 19, pp 183-97.

Blair, S.N., Kohl, H.W., Barlow, C.E., Paffenbarger, R.S., Gibbons, L.W. and Macera, C.A. (1995) 'Changes in physical fitness and all-cause mortality: a prospective study of healthy and unhealthy men', *Journal of the American Medical Association*, vol 273, pp 1093-8.

Booth, T. (1996) 'Sounds of still voices: issues in the use of narrative methods with people who have learning difficulties', in L. Barton (ed) *Disability and society: Emerging issues and insights*, New York, NY: Longman Sociology Series.

Bowker, G. (1993) 'The age of biography is upon us', *Times Higher Education Supplement*, 8 January, p 9.

British Psychological Society (2001) *Code of conduct, ethical principles and guidelines*, Leicester: British Psychological Society.

Brown, S. (1997) 'Excess mortality of schizophrenia: A meta-analysis', *British Journal of Psychiatry*, vol 171, pp 502-8.

Brown, S., Birtwistle, J., Roe, L. and Thompson, C. (1999) 'The unhealthy lifestyle of people with schizophrenia', *Psychological Medicine*, vol 29, pp 697-701.

Bryman, A. (1989) *Research methods and organization studies*, London: Unwin Hyman.

Burbach, F.R. (1997) 'The efficacy of physical activity interventions within mental health services: anxiety and depressive disorders', *Journal of Mental Health*, vol 6, no 6, pp 243-67.

Burchardt, T., Le Grand, J. and Piachaud, D. (2002) 'Degrees of exclusion: developing a dynamic, multidimensional measure', in J. Hills, J. Le Grand and D. Piachaud (eds) *Understanding social exclusion*, New York, NY: Oxford University Press, pp 30-43.

Burgess, R.G. (1984) *In the field: An introduction to field research*, London: Allen and Unwin.

Carr, R. (2002) 'The art of non-verbal communication', *Printmaking Today*, Spring, pp 30-1.

Daumit, G.L., Clark, J.M., Steinwachs, D.M., Graham, C.M., Lehman, A. and Ford, D.E. (2003) 'Prevalence and correlates of obesity in a community sample of individuals with severe and persistent mental illness', *Journal of Nervous and Mental Disease*, vol 191, no 12, pp 799-805.

Donaldson, P. (2001) 'Using photographs to strengthen family planning research', *Family Planning Perspectives*, vol 33, no 4 (www.agi-usa.org/pubs/journals/3317601.html).

Dooley, D. (2003) 'Unemployment, underemployment, and mental health: conceptualizing employment status as a continuum', *American Journal of Community Psychology*, vol 32, nos 1-2, pp 9-20.

Egan, M. and Delaat, M.D. (1994) 'Considering spirituality in occupational therapy practice', *Canadian Journal of Occupational Therapy*, vol 61, no 2, pp 95-101.

Erikssen, G., Liestøl, K., Bjørnhold, J., Thaulow, E., Sandvik, L. and Erikssen, J. (1998) 'Changes in physical fitness and changes in mortality', *Lancet*, vol 352, pp 759-62.

Fieldhouse, J. (2003) 'The impact of an allotment group on mental health clients' well being, and social networking', *British Journal of Occupational Therapy*, vol I66, no 7, pp 286-96.

Fredrickson, L.A. and Anderson, D.H. (1999) 'A qualitative exploration of the wilderness experience as a source of spiritual inspiration', *Journal of Environmental Psychology*, vol 19, no 1, pp 21-39.

Friedenreich, C.M. (2001) 'Physical activity and cancer prevention: from observational to intervention research', *Cancer Epidemiology, Biomarkers and Prevention*, vol 10, pp 287-301.

Friedland, D.S. and Price, R.H. (2003) 'Underemployment: consequences for the health and well-being of workers', *American Journal of Community Psychology*, vol 32, nos 1-2, pp 33-45.

Frumkin, H. (2004) 'White coats, green plants: clinical epidemiology meets horticulture', *Acta Horticulturae*, vol 639, pp 15-25.

Fryer, D. and Payne, R. (1986) 'Being unemployed: a review of the literature on the psychological experience of unemployment', in C.L. Cooper and I. Robertson (eds) *International Review of Industrial and Organizational Psychology*, London: John Wiley & Sons, pp 235-78.

Goodley, D. and Moore, M. (2000) 'Doing disability research: activist lives and the Academy', *Disability and Society*, vol 15, no 6, pp 861-82.

Grimshaw, R. and King, J. (2003) *Horticulture in secure settings*, Reading/London: Thrive/King's College London, Centre for Crime and Justice Studies.

Growth Point (1999) 'Your future starts here: practitioners determine the way ahead', *Growth Point*, vol 79, pp 4-5.

Haddock, G., Slade, P.D., Bentall, R.P., Reid, D. and Faragher, E.B. (1998) 'A comparison of the long-term effectiveness of distraction and focusing in the treatment of auditory hallucinations', *British Journal of Medical Psychology*, vol 71, Part 3, September, pp 339-49.

Hardman, A.E. and Stensel, D.J. (2003) *Physical activity and health: The evidence explained*, London: Routledge.

Harris, E.C. and Barraclough, B. (1998) 'Excess mortality of mental disorder', *British Journal of Psychiatry*, vol 173, pp 11-53.

Hartig, T., Evans, G.W., Jamner, L.J., Davis, D.S. and Gärling, T. (2003) 'Tracking restoration in natural and urban field settings', *Journal of Environmental Psychology*, vol 23, pp 109-23.

Heliker, D., Chadwick, A. and O'Connell, T. (2000) 'The meaning of gardening and the effects on perceived well being of a gardening project on diverse populations of elders', *Activities, Adaptation and Aging*, vol 25, no 3, pp 35-57.

Howard, B.S. and Howard, J.R. (1997) 'Occupation as spiritual activity', *American Journal of Occupational Therapy*, vol 51, no 3, pp 181-5.

Hyer, L., Boyd, S., Scurfield, R., Smith, D. and Burke, J. (1996) 'Effects of outward bound experience as an adjunct to inpatient PTSD treatment of war veterans', *Journal of Clinical Psychology*, vol 52, no 3, pp 263-78.

Jadad, A.R. (ed) (1998) *Randomised controlled trials*, London: BMJ Books.

Jahoda, M. (1979) 'The impact of employment in the 1930s and the 1970s', *Bulletin of the British Psychological Society*, vol 32, pp 309-14.

Kaplan, R. and Kaplan, S. (1989) *The experience of nature: A psychological perspective*, New York, NY: Cambridge University Press.

Kaplan, S. (1995) 'The restorative benefits of nature: toward an integrative framework', *Journal of Environmental Psychology*, vol 15, pp 169-82.

Kellaway, D. (ed) (1996) *The Virago book of women gardeners*, London: Virago Press.

Lakin, C. (1997), 'Rethinking intelligence and creative expression', *Impact*, vol 10, no 1, pp 4-5.

Lindenmuth, G.F. and Moose, B. (1990) 'Improving cognitive abilities of elderly Alzheimer's patients with intense exercise therapy', *The American Journal of Alzheimer's Care and Related Disorders and Research*, vol 5, no 1, pp 31-3.

McSherry, W. and Cash, K. (2004) 'The language of spirituality: an emerging taxonomy', *International Journal of Nursing Studies*, vol 41, pp 151-61.

Measor, L. (1985) 'Interviewing: a strategy in qualitative research', in R.G. Burgess (ed) *Strategies of educational research: Qualitative methods*, London: Falmer Press, pp 55-77.

Milligan, C., Bingley, A. and Gatrell, A. (2003) *Cultivating health: A study of health and mental well-being amongst older people in Northern England*, Lancaster: Institute for Health Research, Lancaster University.

Morse, N.C. and Weiss, R.S. (1955) 'The function and meaning of work and the job', *American Sociological Review*, vol 20, pp 191-8.

Naidoo, J., de Viggiani, N. and Jones, M. (2001) *Making our network more diverse: Black and minority ethnic groups' involvement with gardening projects*, Reading/Bristol, Thrive/University of the West of England.

NEHGDG (North of England Hypertension Guideline Development Group) (2004) *Essential hypertension: Managing adult patients in primary care*, Centre for Health Services Research Report No 111, Newcastle: University of Newcastle upon Tyne.

Netten, A., Rees, A. and Harrison, G. (2001) *Unit costs of health and social care: 2001*, Canterbury: Personal Social Services Research Unit, University of Kent at Canterbury (www.pssru.ac.uk/pdf/UC2001/UnitCosts2001ALL.pdf).

Peel, L. (2004) 'Gaining informed consent', in S. Becker and A. Bryman (eds) *Understanding research methods for social policy and practice*, Bristol: The Policy Press, pp 156-8.

Perkins, R. and Rinaldi, M. (2002) 'Unemployment rates among patients with long-term mental health problems: a decade of rising unemployment', *Psychiatric Bulletin*, vol 26, no 8, pp 295-8.

Perrins-Margalis, N.M., Rugletic, J., Schepis, N.M., Stepanski, H.R. and Walsh, M.A. (2000) 'The immediate effects of a group-based horticulture experience on the quality of life of persons with chronic mental illness', *Occupational Therapy in Mental Health*, vol 16, no 1, pp 15-32.

Powch, I.G. (1994) 'Wilderness therapy: what makes it empowering for women?', *Women and Therapy*, vol 15, nos 3-4, pp 11-27.

Prentice, A.M. and Jeb, S.A. (1995) 'Obesity in Britain: gluttony or sloth?', *British Medical Journal*, vol 311, pp 437-9.

Radley, A. and Taylor, D. (2003) 'Images of recovery: a photo elicitation study on the hospital ward', *Qualitative Health Research*, vol 13, no 1, pp 77-99.

Raine, C. (1994) *History: The home movie: A novel in verse*, New York, NY: Doubleday.

Relf, D. (ed) (2004) *Expanding roles for horticulture in improving human well-being and life quality*, Proceedings of the XXVI International Horticultural Congress, *Acta Horticulturae* 639.

Reynolds, V. (1999) *The Green Gym: An evaluation of a pilot project in Sonning Common, Oxfordshire*, Report no 8, Oxford: Oxford Brookes University.

Reynolds, V. (2002) *Well-being comes naturally: An evaluation of the BTCV Green Gym at Portslade, East Sussex*, Report no 17, Oxford: Oxford Brookes University.

Rosenberg, M. (1965) *Society and the adolescent self-image*, Princeton, NJ: Princeton University Press.

Schwartz, T.L., Nihalani, N., Jindal, S., Virk, S. and Jones, N. (2004) 'Psychiatric medication-induced obesity: a review', *Obesity Reviews*, vol 5, no 2, pp 115-21.

Seller, J., Fieldhouse, J. and Phelan, M. (1999) 'Fertile imaginations: an inner city allotment group', *Psychiatric Bulletin*, vol 23, no 3, pp 291-3.

Sempik, J., Aldridge, J. and Becker, S. (2003) *Social and therapeutic horticulture: Evidence and messages from research*, Reading/Loughborough: Thrive/Centre for Child and Family Research.

Sempik, J., Aldridge, J. and Becker, S. (2005) *Growing together: A practice guide to promoting social inclusion through gardening and horticulture*, Bristol: The Policy Press.

Son, K.C., Song, J.E., Um, S.J., Lee, J.S. and Kwack, H.R. (2004) 'Effects of visual recognition of green plants on the changes of EEG in patients with schizophrenia', *Acta Horticulturae*, vol 639, pp 193-9.

Stigsdotter, U.A. and Grahn, P. (2004) 'A garden at your doorstep may reduce stress: private gardens as restorative environments in the city', Paper 15, Proceedings of the 'Open Space: People Space' Conference on Inclusive Outdoor Environments, Edinburgh, October.

Strauss, D. and Gabaldo, M. (1998) 'Traumatic brain injury and horticultural therapy practice', in S.P. Simson and M.C. Straus (eds) *Horticulture as therapy: Principles and practice*, New York, NY: The Food Products Press/ The Haworth Press, Inc, pp 105-30.

Thun, M. (translated by M. Barton) (1999) *Gardening for life: The biodynamic way*, Stroud: Hawthorn Press.

Unruh, A.M. (2004) 'The meaning of gardens and gardening in daily life: a comparison between gardeners with serious health problems and healthy participants', *Acta Horticulturae*, vol 639, pp 67-73.

Unruh, A.M., Smith, N. and Scammell, C. (2000) 'The occupation of gardening in life-threatening illness: a qualitative pilot project', *Canadian Journal of Occupational Therapy*, vol 67, no 1, pp 70-7.

USDHHS (US Department of Health and Human Services) (1996) *Physical activity and health: A report of the Surgeon General*, Atlanta: USDHHS, Centers for Disease Control and Prevention, National Center for Chronic Disease Prevention and Health Promotion.

Vecchio, R.P. (1980) 'The function and meaning of work and the job: Morse and Weiss (1955) revisited', *Academy of Management Journal*, vol 23, pp 361-7.

Walmsley, J. and Johnson, K. (2003) *Inclusive research with people with learning difficulties*, London: Jessica Kingsley.

Ward, L. (2004) 'Researching vulnerable groups', in S. Becker and A. Bryman (eds) *Understanding research methods for social policy and practice*, Bristol: The Policy Press, pp 169-76.

Ward Thompson, C. (2004) 'Playful nature(s)', Proceedings of the 'Open Space: People space' Conference on Inclusive Outdoor Environments, October, Edinburgh.

Ware, J.E., Snow, K.K., Kosinski, M. and Keller, S.D. (1995) *How to score the SF-12 Physical and Mental Health Summary Scales*, Boston, MA: The Health Institute.

Warr, P.B. (1987) *Work, unemployment and mental health*, Oxford: Oxford Science Publications.

Wichrowski, M., Chambers, N. and Ciccantelli, L. (1998) 'Stroke, spinal chord, and physical disabilities and horticultural therapy practice', in S.P. Simson and M.C. Straus (eds) *Horticulture as therapy: Principles and practice*, New York, NY: The Food Products Press/The Haworth Press, Inc, pp 71-104.

Williams, J.M.G. (1992) *Psychological treatment of depression*, London: Routledge.

Wright, H. (2003) *Biodynamic gardening for health and taste*, London: Mitchell Beazley.

Yamane, K., Kawashima, M., Fujishige, N. and Yoshida, M. (2004) 'Effects of interior horticultural activities with potted plants on human physiological and emotional status', *Acta Horticulturae*, vol 639, pp 37-43.